Talent Shows

the Kent Way

HOW TO PUT TOGETHER AN EXCITING, ENTERTAINING SHOW FEATURING CHILDREN

Talent Shows

the Kent Way

TIPS FOR SHOW COORDINATORS, DIRECTORS, PERFORMERS & STAGE CREWS
A STEP-BY-STEP BEGINNERS GUIDE

BY VARIETY SHOW EXPERTS
Jackie & Danny Kent

Illustrations by Michael Hatch

iUniverse, Inc.

New York Lincoln Shanghai

Talent Shows the Kent Way
HOW TO PUT TOGETHER AN EXCITING, ENTERTAINING SHOW
FEATURING CHILDREN

iUniverse, Inc.

For information address:
iUniverse, Inc.
2021 Pine Lake Road, Suite 100
Lincoln, NE 68512
www.iuniverse.com

ISBN: 0-595-29486-3

Printed in the United States of America

For Mama
Beatrice Hitchin Pheby
It is with great love and respect that we dedicate this work to you.
Thank you for your gentle power and enduring strength.

ACKNOWLEDGEMENTS:

We gratefully thank and acknowledge our producers and show coordinators. Many of them worked with us for five or more years.

OUR PRODUCERS:

Shirley Helleis
Officer Carol Torres
Sam Snyder
Jerry January
Frederick Boldt
Karen Neill
Jewel Hall
Leigh Vizzier
Brad Johnson
Dr. Alice Rodriquez
Dee Ibarra
Carol Smith
Gay Armstrong
Shannon Young
Joanna Allred
Dr. William Hall
Lynda L. Holly
Antonia Hicks
Mary Ellen Phillips
Bonnie Bantis
Tony Gonzales
Robin Sierra
Leslie Bunker
Anna Goodwin
Patricia Roth
Sandy Rosalia
Karen Crabtree
Frank Murphy
Jane Loveday

Dr. Robert Montgomery
Joan Gutierrez
Jack Geving
Paul Yap
Mimi January
Vera Madison
Ruth Ann Walker
Jennifer Walters
Shannon Greenlee
Kay Pittman
Phil Smith
Karen Bennett
Don Wyenberg
Dr. E. DeGarmo
K. L. Hamdorf
Tammy Jansen
Grace Mackin
Mary Anne Flood
Chris Ross
Maggie Kentro
Martina Rodriguez
Emily Lucy
John R. Madsen
Debbie Silver
Pat Hill
Susan Cunningham
Linda Chester
Pat Ricci
Tom Crellin

Dr. Frances Read
Margie Foelber
Dr. Cheryl Cox
Newton Hamilton
A. Walters
Sandy Dempewolf
Charles Ernst
Deena Holcomb
Carol Mallow
Georgia Ardelt
Frank Peterson
Frank Murphy
John Pletcher
Peg Cowman
Grace Sherr
Peggy Sammons
Robin Tobiasson
Ray Cannavino
John Weld
Chris Garcia
Evelyn Tate
Ed Stokes
Judy Cartwright
John Nelson
Debbie Rinehart
Dr. Arlan Hurt
Lynne Tarola
Phyllis Johnstone
Nancy Yates

Dawn Gutierrez
Suzanne Freeman
Wendy Fougeron
Ruth Ann Walker
Sally Kaufman
Stewart Brown
Dee Ibarra
Dana Markert
Arlene Nelson
Mary Louise Martin

Jo Davis
Cathy Bender
Pat Karlsgodt
Harriet Vale
Bonnie McGrath
Steve Pollett
Darlene Cason
Lyle Rangel
Kay Pittman
Sue Yakabik

Tanya Chen
Linda Ashley
Albert Mendivil
Linda Rodriguez
Don Jeffries
Patsy Minezaki
Clifford Mendoza
Jan Perdue
Allen Blair
George Bjornstad

OUR SHOW COORDINATORS:

John & Margaret Pietrzak
Dick Slaker
Sue Miller
Judy Mattei
Judy Parker
Jennifer Kvalvik
Diane Gustafson
Edie Odierno
Teresa Moran
Debbie Brunick
Jane Lee
Wayne & Vicki Riggs
Barbara La Shell
Bonnie Hayman
Mary Lou Garcia
Rose Hernandez
Margaret Verrilli
Judy Parker
Ernestine Thornton
Laurie Vierra
Susan Guidry
Pat Miller
Darlene Montgomery
Karl & Leslie Bunker
Charlotte Sachtjen
Chris Garcia
Selena Carter

Joan Gutierrez
Maxine Mercer
Carole Sabin
Linda Holly
Helen Steel
Barbara Boucher
Cheryl Kies
Pam Craig
Rick Wall
Linda Brown
Bob Thompson
John & Vicki Freese
Bonnie Taylor
Vinnie Thoms
Debbie LeRoy
Peggy Araujo
Veronica Roland
Jean Howard
Charlotte Williams
Elaine Ingham
Jayne Barrena
Wendy Fourgeron
Carol Collinson
Yvonne Perry
Darcy Jaime
Roger Cunningham
Debbie Rinehart

Jo Davis
Judy Backhaus
Denise Bohling
Diane Sanchez
Linda Rayburn
Barbara Grider
Joyce Dirksen
Pepper Sutton
Butch Elliot
E. J. Valdez
Linda Coughburn
Roberta Horne
Roy Shepherd
Sharon Pecoraro
Sherri Rowell
Linda Culpeper
Linda Smyth
Sylvia Cornette
Carol Marbrey
Tammy Gibson
Shauna Ahiers
Kathy Smith
Barbara Garza
Maria Zadorozny
Sandy Rosalia
Mrs. Holmquist
Terrie Watton

Linda Chester
Sandi Killalea
Robin Siota

Francie Collins
Edie Odierno
Helen Steel

Cheryl Kies
Sally Kaufman

*And last but not least, we acknowledge all of the performers and crew members
who shared the adventure with us, including our daughters,
Linda, Lizette and Madeleine.
Thank you for your energy, your brilliance and your valiant spirits.
Play on!*

CONTENTS

ILLUSTRATIONS BY MICHAEL HATCH

INTRODUCTION

YOU CAN DO IT!
WE'LL SHOW YOU HOW

WHAT IS THE KENT WAY?

The Kent way is a reliable, tried-and-true method that encourages self-expression and creativity.

    It's time-effective; only two rehearsals are required

    Everyone who auditions gets to be in the show

    Everyone is a winner; it's not a competition

The substance of each act is contributed from a great variety of sources:

    Family members

    Performing arts studios

    The performers themselves…

It is the director's job to make sure that each act has a strong beginning, a definite ending and is the ideal length. *"Always leave 'em wanting more!"*

WHO ARE YOUR PERFORMERS?

    Children

    Children and parents together

    Guest artists of all ages

HOW LONG DOES IT TAKE TO PUT A SHOW TOGETHER?

4 weeks before performance time:	ANNOUNCE YOUR SHOW
8 days before performance time:	HOLD AUDITIONS
3 days before performance time:	MEET WITH YOUR CREW
2 days before performance time:	REHEARSE
1 day before performance time:	REHEARSE

WHO PUTS IT TOGETHER AND DELEGATES?

✓ Someone Just Like You!

✓ A Parent or Guardian

✓ A Grandparent

✓ Church Youth Group Leaders
✓ The PTA (Parent-Teacher Association)
✓ Summer Camp Counselors
✓ Recreation Center Directors
✓ Resource Teachers
✓ School Principals
✓ Police Department School Safety Patrol Advisors
✓ Corporate Event Organizers
✓ Entertainment Planning Committees…

EASY-TO-LEARN THEATRICAL TECHNIQUES:

This introduction to live theater, offers a training ground where budding singers, song-writers, poets, actors, joke-writers, fashion designers, dancers, choreographers, and a multitude of other creative people, can learn the fundamentals of what it takes to perform in front of an audience or behind the scenes in the crew.

Whether we're giving a report, making a presentation, accepting an award, applying for a job or asking the boss for a raise, the earlier in life that we learn to express ourselves confidently, the better.

We invite you to gain from our experience.

With love and best wishes,

Jackie & Danny Kent

CHAPTER ONE

WHY? 10 POWERFUL REASONS

POWERFUL REASON #1: BUILDS SELF-ESTEEM

In our experience as directors (well over 15,000 students have participated in our performance/workshops) we have observed that:

Children clearly thrive and flourish on acknowledgement, validation and appreciation.

It is very important to place children in situations where they can succeed and feel good about themselves.

"I noticed that even after two weeks, those who had participated were more self-confident, projected their personalities better in front of the student body, and in general felt very good about themselves. One student in particular needed the positive reinforcement that the Kents provided. A week earlier, he had run away from school. Now, he waves and smiles at me!"

JUDY MATTEI—PARENT—SHOW COORDINATOR
Hickman Elementary School, San Diego, CA

"The show gave us a chance to be somebody we've always wanted to be."
ADAM—Age 10—Martial Arts Demonstrator

"The Kents' professional coaching, organization and inspiration all contribute to a learning situation with polished flair. The children begin with a desire to be on the stage; they conclude with applause from an appreciative audience. For some children the desire is greater than the skill, but through the Kents' coaching, I have seen a second-grader clutching a jump rope blossom into a skipper accompanied by appropriate music. The delight shows on the faces of the participants and the audience. Each show has been a winner with a packed house."

DR. FRANCES READ—PRINCIPAL
Feaster Elementary School, Chula Vista, CA

POWERFUL REASON #2: CELEBRATES INDIVIDUALITY

Often, after watching music videos and trying out moves in front of a mirror at home, kids put their own routines together.

We have found that shows, in which none of the acts had taken private lessons, have been just as successful as shows in which many of the performers were professionally trained. Sparkle, energy, poise and enthusiasm are the things that please the audience. *It's not what you do; it's the way that you do it!*

"Being in the show gives you a chance to do what you're good at!"
      TANEYA—Age 8—Dancer

POWERFUL REASON #3: BRINGS FAMILIES TOGETHER

Brothers, sisters, aunts, uncles, parents and grandparents often play a major role in getting a child ready to audition and perform. They help by choosing music, costumes, teaching lyrics, dance steps, magic tricks...

In addition to bringing families together, *Talent Shows the Kent Way* provides children with an opportunity to share their culture with fellow-students. When children do a song or dance from a relative's native land, it adds a splendid texture to the show. Some of our shows have included songs and dances from Vietnam, Laos, Cambodia, Mexico, Iran, Ireland, Cuba, Africa, India, the Philippines and others.

Friends and relatives sometimes come up with very unusual ideas. On one show a girl spun a hula-hoop while playing "*The Yellow Rose of Texas*" on the violin.

POWERFUL REASON #4: BUILDS CHARACTER

Some of the objectives of *Talent Shows the Kent Way* are:
      Widen interests
      Overcome shyness and stage fright
      Keep a promise and follow through
      Acquire poise
      Learn the value of punctuality
      Develop trust in others
      Experience the power and success of teamwork.

POWERFUL REASON #5: BUILDS TEAM SPIRIT

There soon develops within the cast and crew an esprit de corps; that wonderful feeling of truly belonging.

POWERFUL REASON #6: PROVIDES A FORUM FOR SELF EXPRESSION

Freedom of expression is as precious to a child as it is to an adult.

In one of our shows, a boy with artistic ability did a drawing. We supplied him with an easel, a 2'x 3' drawing pad and a heavy black marker. He liked the Disney movie *"The Little Mermaid"* and did a beautiful cartoon of her while the audience watched. They loved it. His mother wrote: *"Thank you for giving my son an opportunity to be on the stage and draw before an audience. It earned him a lot of recognition among his peers."*

POWERFUL REASON #7: UNIFIES THE COMMUNITY

The Master/Mistress of Ceremonies (MC) when introducing each act to the audience, acknowledges the numerous people in the community who may have helped performers prepare:

Family members
Friends
Dance studios
Private music teachers
Band directors
Martial arts instructors
Art teachers
Voice and drama coaches
Gymnastics coaches
Baton-twirling instructors
Comedy coaches…
(Some of the funniest jokes and comedy sketches on our shows have been contributed and coached by camp counselors and family members.)

"I'm glad I was able to participate in it. It was really enjoyable and I was glad when you gave me all those reassuring 'good lucks and the good jobs' at the show. I will remember you two forever. Thanks."
DANIEL—Age 11—Master of Ceremonies

POWERFUL REASON #8: PROVIDES EDUCATIONAL BENEFITS

Sharpens reading skills
Improves speech
Provides children with an opportunity to acquire an early appreciation for theater
Students experience how theatrical action depends on oral, visual and musical cues.

POWERFUL REASON #9: MOTIVATES CHILDREN TO PURSUE ADVANCED LEARNING

"Many students have been motivated to go on to advanced learning in the areas of music and drama at the university level due to experience and encouragement given by Jackie and Danny Kent. They are first-rate!"
SHIRLEY HELLEIS—PRINCIPAL
Allen School, Bonita, CA

POWERFUL REASON # 10: RAISES FUNDS FOR A WORTHY CAUSE

"With little advertising, we had a packed house two nights running, not to mention the revenues from concessions. This is one fund raising event where everyone benefits."
SUSAN GUIDRY—PARENT—SHOW COORDINATOR
Casa de Oro Elementary School, Spring Valley, CA

CHAPTER TWO

TALENT SHOWS THE KENT WAY

At an elementary school in San Diego, California, Jason, a five-year-old from morning kindergarten was the next student to audition. We asked him what he wanted to do on the show. In his husky voice he said, **"I'm gonna play the piano."** He climbed up onto the piano bench and started randomly hitting the piano keys with his two index fingers. We waited patiently for a little while, and then asked, *"Jason, which tune would you like to play?"* No answer, just more random notes on the piano. Catching on, we asked, *"Have you ever played the piano before?"* He replied, **"No, but I want to!"** Did Jason "pass" the audition, or was he turned away? At this point, Jason's self-esteem was on the line.

The question we asked ourselves when Jason auditioned was, *"How can we place this child, to show him off to his best advantage?"* Noticing Jason's wonderful speaking voice and his obvious chutzpah, we cast him in a comedy sketch and he performed magnificently!

A TYPICAL SHOW:

It's show time! Your performers and crew are prepared and ready! After only two rehearsals your kids radiate a beautiful confidence.

At the entrance to the auditorium, family and friends stream in and friendly ushers are taking tickets and handing out programs.

Inside, the auditorium is set up with chairs separated by an aisle down the center. Along one of the side walls are two rows of benches where the excited performers are seated. Yes, the *green-room* is in the audience. There is an excited buzz as the performers eagerly wait for their chance in the spotlight and parents and friends prepare their video cameras.

The energy is high, there is a charged feeling in the air, and your close-knit team is about to enjoy the rewards of their efforts in the form of warm smiles and enthusiastic applause!

At seven o'clock the show's producer welcomes the audience and says how great it feels to have a packed house and mentions that the revenues generated from ticket sales will be used to buy some much-needed equipment. Your producer then introduces your MC. The follow-spotlight goes on, the house lights dim, and the MC takes over.

Your MC has learned the importance of being a gracious host and emits a powerful command presence.

Your crew of eleven to eighteen-year-olds is very capable and takes great pride in their jobs, knowing that their alertness and careful attention to the task at hand is crucial to the success of the show.

The MC reads the cue for the first act: *"Let's get the show started with a group coached by Antonio Gomez. Please open the curtain for "THE GOMEZ GYM-NASTS!"* The crew with precision responds to this cue or trigger phrase, The Gomez Gymnasts. It's like throwing a power switch that sets everything in motion. Instantaneously, some fast music starts as the curtain opens to a lit stage. The act is an attention-getter and creates a great deal of excitement.

At the conclusion of each act the MC re-enters immediately, waits amiably for the applause to diminish, then introduces the next act. The second act is a lively dancer in a colorful costume, and the third act is comedy.

By this time, your show is really rolling and the audience is relaxed and happy. Your show is lined-up beautifully and includes an abundance of variety.

The first act is energetic and features a group of children who work to fast, exhilarating music. The second act is a dancer (perhaps hip-hop, tap or Tahitian) who is also very energetic but his or her choice of music contrasts strongly to the previous act. The third act, a comedian, uses no music and provides laughter.

Your show consists of between twenty-four and thirty acts (about seventy-five to one hundred people) and is about an hour long. The pacing is excellent and your production subtly builds in momentum to your closing act. (See Chapter 8—*How to Line Up Your Show*).

After the last act has performed, the MC gives credit to the crew and the assisting adults.

Next is the *Finale Parade,* a very delightful feature where all of the performers in succession take a final bow and exit down the center aisle directly through the audience. The director thanks the MC for doing a great job and brings him or her back for a bow. Words of praise and thanks are given to the audience for their presence and help in making the event such a resounding success!

The house lights go on and the radiant performers and crew rush to their proud friends and relatives. There is an expansive feeling of warmth that fills the auditorium. Hugs and complements are everywhere!

IDEAS—A WIDE RANGE OF PERFORMING POSSIBILITIES:

Show off gymnastic skills
Acrobatics
Jump rope; single or double-Dutch
Draw a cartoon
Do a martial arts demonstration
Do magic tricks; slight-of-hand, an illusion…
Be a Mime (a performer who uses silent gestures rather than words)
Twirl a baton
Do a puppet show using hand puppets or marionettes worked by strings
Lead a cheer
Juggle
Rap
Be a ventriloquist (the skill of speaking without moving the lips)
Do a short dramatic scene
Dance; hip-hop, tap, jazz, ballet, swing…
Sing
Be a comic; tell jokes, riddles, do a funny monologue, a short sketch…
Read an excerpt from a favorite poem or story (perhaps one you've written yourself)
Impersonate a famous person; John Wayne, Whoopie Goldberg…
Do an ethnic dance that features a colorful costume and exotic music
Coordinate a fashion show (possibly with fashions you designed and/or constructed yourself)

> Sportswear: Football, tennis, baseball…
> Business attire: Doctor, construction worker…
> Evening wear: Luxurious fabrics, capes, top hats, frills, jewels, feathers…
> Costumes: Vintage, futuristic, super heroes, magic wizards, wild and crazy creations…

CHAPTER THREE

YOUR PRODUCTION TEAM

When you carefully surround yourself with helpful, positive, enthusiastic people, who are willing to provide an atmosphere of safety and acceptance for your courageous performers, you will find that the results can be astounding.

ADULTS ARE REQUIRED FOR THE FOLLOWING POSITIONS:

Producer
Director
Coordinator
Sound technician
Security

PRODUCER:

The producer is in charge of handling revenues and paying expenses.

DIRECTOR:

The director is in charge of the theatrical aspects of the production. His or her primary goal is to put together an entertaining show.

The director's qualifications:
A strong interest in musical theater
Radiates approval
Is enthusiastic
Has a good sense of humor.

The director's duties:
Sets up media coverage
Screens the lyrics to all songs and the content of all spoken material
Holds MC (Master/Mistress of Ceremonies) try-outs
Auditions performers

Decides on the length of each act
Lines up the show (establishes the order of appearance of the performers)
Writes the cue sheet (a list of introductions)
Creates the technical worksheet
Instructs the crew
Directs the rehearsals
Provides constant support and encouragement.

COORDINATOR:

The show coordinator works as liaison between the producer and director and is in charge of the administrative tasks.

The coordinator's duties:
Arranges for the printing of:
    The announcement
    The sign-up sheets
    The request for crew and MC candidates form
    Tickets
    Programs
Borrows or rents equipment such as:
    The follow-spotlight (optional)
Appoints volunteers:
    Ushers
    Video camera operator
    Security
    Refreshment sales (optional)
    Souvenir sales (optional)
Distributes:
    The announcement
Distributes and collects:
    The sign-up sheets
    Request for stage crew/MC candidates' form.

SOUND TECHNICIAN:

The sound technician's qualifications:
General knowledge of electronics
Musical aptitude
Encouraging attitude.

The sound technician's duties:
Sets up and tests sound equipment
Monitors and adjusts sound levels *(constant alertness is required)*
Cues up and starts tapes

At rehearsals and/or whenever live accompanists are not available, cassette tapes are used. *(See Precision Cueing—Chapter 7).*

SECURITY:

The casual presence of two adults is advised in two areas:

1. *Backstage*:
   On a few occasions our stage managers and performers have been bothered by kids who managed to get backstage undetected. The mere presence of an authoritative figure will discourage this mischief.

   It should be understood between security and the stage manager that security is there only for emergencies and should not get involved with any backstage business. The crew is well rehearsed and takes pride in being in command of their jobs.

2. *The follow-spotlight location*:
   The follow-spotlight arouses curiosity and the area surrounding it can become a social center. The spotlight operators need protection from being crowded by audience members. Their space should be maintained so that they can do their jobs properly.

CHILDREN AGES ELEVEN TO EIGHTEEN DO VERY WELL AS:

Master or mistress of ceremonies
MC understudy/sound technician's assistant
Stage manager
Green-room supervisors
Follow-spotlight operators
Curtain operator

MASTER/MISTRESS OF CEREMONIES (MC):

Qualifications:
Reading ability
Clear speech

Enthusiasm
A good sense of humor.

Duties:
Introduces each act to the audience in succession
Acknowledges the producer and assisting adults
Brings the crew out for a bow
Introduces the finale parade.

MC UNDERSTUDY/SOUND TECHNICIAN'S ASSISTANT:

Qualifications:
Same as the MC—listed above.

Duties:
Takes over for the MC when required
Introduces the MC's act (if the MC is performing)
Assists the sound technician by setting up microphones, as previously rehearsed by the director.

STAGE MANAGER:

Qualifications:
Leadership ability
Warm-heartedness (toward nervous performers who are waiting to go on stage.)

Duties:
Checks to see that all props are accounted for
Places props swiftly and accurately (as previously rehearsed by the director)
Maintains quiet and order backstage.

THREE GREEN-ROOM SUPERVISORS:

Qualifications:
Alertness
Leadership ability
A cheerful, encouraging attitude.

Duties:
Takes performer attendance
Supervises quiet, prompt, performer traffic from the green-room to the stage and back.

TWO FOLLOW-SPOTLIGHT OPERATORS:

Qualifications:
A sense of visual proportion
Alertness

CURTAIN OPERATOR:

Qualifications:
Prompt response to cues
Encouraging attitude
Duties:
Opens and closes the curtain smoothly and precisely (as previously rehearsed by the director).

CHAPTER FOUR

COMPACT SCHEDULING

"I liked the way it was almost perfect with only two practices."
  NOELIA—Age 9—Vocalist

ONLY TWO REHEARSALS ARE REQUIRED:

A compact schedule spurs a certain momentum and keeps the director's instructions fresh in the minds of the performers and crew.

THE TIME LINE:

4 weeks before performance time:	*Distribute:*
	The Show Announcement/Sign-up Sheets
	Request for Crew/MC Candidate Form
	Send:
	Press release to media
8 days before performance time:	*Hold Auditions*
3 days before performance time:	*Meet with your crew*
2 days before performance time	*Rehearse*
1 day before performance time	*Rehearse*

REHEARSAL #1:

The first rehearsal takes place a week or so after the audition. At this rehearsal, students are taught the fundamentals of theatrical communication.

REHEARSAL #2:

It is essential that the second rehearsal takes place the day after the first rehearsal. The goal of this rehearsal is to get performers accustomed to the *uninterrupted pace* of the show. At this rehearsal the whole show is done in sequence, and up to speed.

SCHOOL SHOWS—EDUCATIONAL VALUE:

When scheduling school shows, principals usually agree that the educational value of *Talent Shows the Kent Way* justifies having the production sessions during school time.

"I particularly appreciated the care and guidance that the Kents provided patiently, for the children assisting them in the development of their performances with taping of music and the direction of performance content. They also made it possible for students to be involved with all aspects of the variety show (lighting, stage-hands, narrator, etc.) I have found that shows produced with the Kents' assistance have proven to be a valuable educational experience. Oral language, music, drama and dance are among those areas especially highlighted."

DR. ROBERT MONTGOMERY, PRINCIPAL
Halecrest Elementary School, Chula Vista, CA

SCHEDULING REHEARSALS:

When scheduling rehearsals, be on the alert for in-school conflicts such as:
Classes away on field trips
District-wide testing…

STUDENTS SPEND A MINIMUM AMOUNT OF TIME OUT OF CLASS:

Audition:
Students are brought to the auditorium by the green-room supervisors a few at a time. After the performers have auditioned, they are sent back to class immediately.

First Rehearsal:
The school-show first rehearsal is divided into *three* parts; there are approximately eight acts in each part. After each act rehearses, they are sent back to class.

Second Rehearsal:
All of the performers stay for the entire rehearsal.

A SUGGESTED SCHOOL SHOW FIRST REHEARSAL SCHEDULE:

1. The performers in the first third of the show attend the first session; in the morning, immediately after roll-call.
2. The performers in the middle third of the show attend the second session, after morning recess.
3. The remaining performers attend the final session, after lunch.

Acts with the most people in them, within each segment, rehearse first (out of sequence) so that a larger number of students can be sent back to class sooner.

BEST DAYS TO SCHEDULE EVENING PERFORMANCES:

When scheduling school shows, we have found that Wednesdays and Thursdays are best for evening performances. Friday evening is the start of the weekend and people will not usually attend school functions on that night.

AN IDEAL SCHOOL SHOW SCHEDULE		
SESSION	DAY OF WEEK	TIME REQUIRED
Audition	Monday	About 3 hours
First Rehearsal	Tuesday—*8 days later*	Most of the school day
Second Rehearsal	Wednesday	About 3 hours
First Evening Performance	Wednesday 7 PM	About 1 hour
First Assembly *(Lower grades)*	Thursday morning	About 1 hour
Second Evening Performance	Thursday 7 PM	About 1 hour
Second Assembly *(Upper grades)*	Friday morning	About 1 hour

AN IDEAL ALL-PURPOSE SCHEDULE

SESSION	DAY OF WEEK	TIME REQUIRED
Audition	Monday 6 PM	About 3 hours
First Rehearsal Part 1—The performers, who are in the first half of the show, attend this session.	Tuesday 6 PM *(8 days later)*	About 3 hours
First Rehearsal Part 2—The performers, who are in the second half of the show, attend this session.	Wednesday 6 PM	About 3 hours
Second Rehearsal—The entire cast attends this rehearsal.	Thursday 6 PM	About 3 hours
First Performance	Friday 7 PM	About 1 hour
Second Performance	Saturday 7 PM	About 1 hour
Third Performance	Sunday 2 PM Matinee	About 1 hour

INTERMISSION:

We suggest that you do not break for an intermission, as it would disrupt the momentum of the show. The show is only about an hour in length. Refreshments could be served before and/or after the performance.

CHAPTER FIVE

CHOOSING YOUR LOCATION

If at all possible, choose an indoor location so that weather conditions are not a problem.

CHOICE OF VENUES:

Auditorium
Multi-Purpose Room
Town Hall
Church Hall
Theater
Recreation Center
Gymnasium...

AVAILABILITY:

The same location is needed for both rehearsals and all performances.

The audition can be held elsewhere; in any large room that has a piano and a good floor for dancers.

VISIBILITY:

When the audience is seated flat on the floor on the same level as your performers, the view of audience members (seated in the third row and beyond) is obstructed by the people who are sitting in front of them. This makes it difficult or impossible for them to see the lower portion of:

Comedians who are doing funny antics close to the floor
Dancers, gymnasts, rope skippers, etc., whose foot and legwork is an integral part of their presentation.

Therefore, it is best to choose a venue that either has a stage that elevates your performers or sloped seating that gradually elevates the audience.

STAGE FLOOR:

Tap, clog and flamenco dancing, in particular, require a smooth, responsive floor.

If your performing area is *carpeted*, as it is in most multi-purpose rooms, and you have one or more of the above types of dance acts on your show, you may want to place sheets of plywood on the carpet and tape them together with strong, wide tape, so that they won't separate or shift.

If your performance site is a gymnasium and the floor must be protected from tap-shoes etc., the above suggestion could provide a quick and simple solution.

WINGS:

The wings are narrow curtains or flats at the sides of the stage.

Wings create concealed places where performers stand while they are waiting for their cue to enter.

In venues where there are no side curtains or flats, wings can be created by using screens, partitions or portable chalk boards covered from top to bottom with heavy paper. They should be about six feet high and at least five feet wide.

BACK WALL OR BACKDROP:

A back wall is necessary to limit the depth of the stage and define the performing area. It provides some acoustic reflection of sound waves and creates a backdrop on which performers' shadows can be seen, thus doubling the visual effect. But most of all, a back wall and wings create an enclosed place where completely inexperienced children can perform with confidence.

In outdoor situations where a back wall doesn't exist or in a gymnasium where the back wall is at too great a distance (for this type of event) a backdrop would have to be improvised.

THE SOUND SYSTEM:

Microphones:

> *Talent Shows the Kent Way* usually involve around seventy-five or more performers and move way too fast for complicated microphone set-ups, such as individual cordless microphones. Our experience has shown us that just two well-placed microphones can handle the challenge effectively.

Microphone #1—The MC's microphone is primarily used by the MC and occasionally by:
>Backup singers
>Narrators
>Fashion show coordinators…

Microphone #2—The performer's microphone is used by:
>Vocalists
>Stand-up comics
>Instrumentalists…

Microphone #2 is also utilized when the percussive floor sounds made by various performers require amplification. For example:
>Dancers; clog, flamenco, tap…
>Jugglers; who use ball bouncing as part of their routines
>Rope skippers…

Microphone stands:
Two microphone-stands that raise and lower smoothly to various heights are required. It is necessary to use the type of microphone stand that has a screw-on attachment at the top, sometimes called an *adaptor clip* that the microphone fits into. This attachment makes it possible to remove the microphone from its stand quickly and easily.

An amplifier:
A powered mixer, sometimes called the PA (public address) is the amplifier and controlling center of the PA system. Each input should have its own volume; treble (high), bass (low) and reverberation controls. The reverberation control when used *sensitively*, adds a warm, rich quality to the speaking or singing voice. It's like singing in the shower; the sound quality is improved considerably.

>Input #1:   If your amplifier has special inputs for a tape player, don't use them. Use the channel one microphone input so you can control the tone quality (treble and bass) of the different tapes; *they vary greatly.*
>Input #2:   Is used for the MC's microphone.
>Input #3:   Is used for the performer's microphone.

Loudspeakers:
At least two speakers are required.

LIGHTING:

House lights: Lights in the audience part of a theater or auditorium.
The house lights are on when the audience arrives and remain on until the MC is introduced.

Wall sconces:
Check to see if there is peripheral lighting around the perimeter of your audience space. Soft, ambient lighting, such as wall sconces, that can be left on throughout the entire show (so that the audience is not in total darkness) is ideal.

In addition to being good for safety reasons, this subtle lighting makes it possible for performers to see the friendly faces of their audience; a definite advantage.

Ante-pro lights:
Most auditoriums have spotlights in the ceiling (about fifteen feet back from the front edge of the stage). These lights are called *ante-pro;* meaning in front of the proscenium *(see glossary).*

The ante-pro lights illuminate the *front section* of the stage, and may either be clear or covered with colored gels; alternating red, yellow and blue are best.

Border lights:
In most auditoriums, there is a border of lights behind the front curtain that shines down on, and illuminates the *mid-section* of the stage. Most often, these lights have colored gels attached to them. Again, alternating red, yellow and blue is most effective.

Photoflood lamps:
If your location doesn't have any stage lighting at all, photoflood lamps, set on stands, could be used *(150 watts or higher).* They should be situated on each side of the stage, aimed toward the center of the performing area and placed in such a way that the light doesn't spill out onto the audience.

Follow-spotlight:
Check to see whether or not a follow-spotlight is available at your location. It is advisable to ask for a spare bulb.

A follow-spotlight has the ability to project a bright circle of light that can be enlarged to cover a group of people or reduced to the size of a single person's

head. It focuses attention and can add a very professional quality to your production. If a follow-spotlight is not available at your show site, you may want to borrow or rent one from:
>	An elementary, junior high or high school in your district
>	A local theater group
>	A theatrical lighting company

CURTAIN:

If your performance site has a front curtain, check to see if it glides smoothly as it opens and closes.

In most theaters and auditoriums, the front curtain is set back about six feet from the front edge of the stage. Performing in this area is called, *"working in one"*. This space is used for acts that don't move around much during their routines, such as:
>	Vocalists
>	Stand-up comics
>	Instrumentalists…

The benefits of having performance space in front of the closed curtain:
>	While the previous act is working, the next act can *quietly* be getting into position, behind the closed curtain (unseen by the audience).
>	While one act is performing in front of the closed curtain, the stage manager can be placing props (behind the curtain), for the act that is to follow.

If your show site doesn't have a front curtain, don't be concerned. All set-ups can be done in full view of the audience. (*Set-up precision is discussed in Chapter 10*).

PIANO OR ELECTRONIC KEYBOARD:

You will need a piano that rolls easily. If there is no piano at your location, an electronic keyboard could be brought in for accompanists and featured pianists to play.

STAIRS FOR THE FINALE PARADE:

If your performance site has a stage, stairs will be necessary so that your performers can get from the stage to the auditorium floor during the finale parade. If none are available at your site, stairs will have to be borrowed or built.

When your performers work flat on the floor and the audience is seated on tiered seating (as they are for a gymnasium show) stairs are not needed.

PLATFORM TO ELEVATE THE FOLLOW-SPOTLIGHT:

1.   If you decide to use a follow-spotlight and your performance site does not have a projection booth or balcony, or if audience seating is flat rather than sloped, a platform will be required (so that when audience members stand up, they won't obstruct the light).
2.   If your follow-spotlight is on wheels, a molding around the edge will be necessary to prevent it from rolling off.
3.   Suggested platform measurements: 3' high, 5' wide, 5' deep.

TWO TABLES:

Table #1:   At the audition, both rehearsals and all performances, a 6' long table is needed for the sound technician's use.

Table #2:   A smaller table or student desk is needed at the audition only. (Sign-up sheets are placed on this table.)

COMFORT:

Check on heating and air-conditioning. It's best if your location is a little on the cool side during performances.

AUDIENCE SPACE:

If there is a choice between a facility with a smaller seating capacity and one that is much too big for your anticipated audience, we feel it is better to choose the smaller, friendlier one. A packed house is every producer's dream. It spells success and the audience and performers can definitely feel the difference.

BENCHES OR CHAIRS FOR YOUR GREEN-ROOM:

After you have held your audition, you will be able to determine the number of benches or folding chairs needed for green-room seating.

CHAPTER SIX

AUDITION PREPARATION

NAMING YOUR SHOW:

Choosing a catchy name for your show helps to stimulate interest. We suggest that your title includes either:
1. The name of the corporation, school, church, etc., that is sponsoring or producing your show. For example:
    "The Franklin Frolics"
    "The Cleveland Capers"
    "Bravo For Bancroft"
2. Your sponsoring organization's mascot:
    "The Roadrunner Revue"
    "In Tune With The Tigers"
    "Movin' With The Mustangs".
3. Your sponsoring organization plus the current year, implying a yearly tradition:
    "The Franklin Frolics of 2003".

STORYLINES AND THEMES:

Although some might feel that their show needs to be packaged into a storyline or unified by a theme, we feel it is not necessary to spend the time and effort to superimpose an extraneous theme.
For example:
    Talent Around the World
    Auditions at the Bus Stop

Much of the strength of *Talent Shows the Kent Way* is due to the fact that performers are not conforming to a role. They are doing acts mostly of their own choosing and are being themselves.

EASE OF STAGING:

Furniture or scenery is allowed only if:

It is truly crucial to the situation
It can quickly and easily be placed into position in a matter of seconds.

Experience has shown us that all that is needed are:
A couple of chairs when depicting a waiting room
A table can be used to signify Frankenstein's operating room
A performer playing a nurse in a doctor's office can easily set the scene by wearing a nurse's cap and carrying a clipboard.

COSTUMES:

If a performer has a costume, that's fine. If not, they can wear their regular clothes. The most important thing is that every child has the opportunity to become involved.

For the costume parade it is suggested that participants give their imaginations full reign and wear creations put together out of pieces that they, a friend, or someone in their family, already owns.

THE ANNOUNCEMENT AND THE SIGN-UP SHEET:

The announcement and the sign-up sheet are printed back-to-back on the same page. These forms should be given out about four weeks before the audition date so that your performers have enough time to:
Decide on what kind of act they would like to do
Choose music (if desired)
Practice
Find, borrow or sew a costume (if desired).

THE DUE DATE:

Let's suppose that your due date for accepting sign-up sheets has arrived.
The Show Coordinator:
1.   Checks to see if names have been spelled legibly (so that they will be listed on the program correctly).
2.   Checks to see if all questions have been answered as completely as possible, so that the director can provide the MC with something descriptive, fascinating, impressive or unusual to say when introducing each act to the audience.
3.   Checks to see that the words to all songs and spoken material have been written out or photocopied.

The Director:
>   Reviews the overall turn-out
>   Screens material.

>   Lyrics to songs or comedy material might be offensive and therefore unacceptable for one or more of the following reasons:
>>   Obscene
>>   Sacrilegious
>>   Violent
>>   Insulting

In the event that the director, after carefully reviewing the submitted material, finds that it is inappropriate, the performer is given an alternate choice and is recast

TWO SAMPLE SHOWS—A SCHOOL SHOW AND AN ALL-PURPOSE SHOW:

Sample School Show: *The Rogers Revue*

Producer:	Elementary School Principal
Show coordinator:	PTA President
Location:	School Auditorium

An Announcement/Sign-up Sheet is sent home with every student in the school.

Sample All-Purpose Show: *Celebrating Clarksville*

Producer:	Police Department
Show Coordinator:	Police Officer/Safety Patrol Advisor
Location:	Gymnasium

Depending on who is producing or sponsoring your show, an announcement/sign-up sheet is distributed or made available to everyone in that particular group.

Please note:
The forms are basically the same, whether they're for a school show or an all-purpose show.

STEP 1: ANNOUNCE YOUR SHOW

FORM #1—THE TALENT SHOW ANNOUNCEMENT:

Name the form: *Talent Show Announcement*

Name your show: _____

Mention your Producer: _____

Show Coordinator: _____

Director: _____

Address your announcement to your specific group:

        Students

        Corporate employees and their families

        Church youth group…

List performance ideas: See sample form.

Time limit: Acts should be 2 minutes in length or less

Schedule: Dates and times for:

        The Audition _____

        1st Rehearsal _____

        2nd Rehearsal _____

        1st Performance_____

        2nd Performance _____

        3rd Performance_____

Ticket price: Adults_____ Children _____

THE PTA PROUDLY PRESENTS

THE ROGERS REVUE

PRODUCER: PRINCIPAL, SAM GERSHWIN

COORDINATOR: PTA PRESIDENT, TYRA WASHINGTON

DIRECTOR: PARENT, SOPHIA CASTILLANO

ROGERS ELEMENTARY SCHOOL STUDENTS, PARENTS, TEACHERS, OFFICE STAFF, CUSTODIANS

WE INVITE YOU TO SIGN UP AND JOIN THE FUN!

PERFORMANCE SUGGESTIONS – IDEAS
Show off your gymnastic skills - jump rope - do acrobatics - draw a cartoon - do yo-yo tricks - sing - lead a cheer - do a martial arts demonstration - do magic tricks - be a mime - twirl a baton - do a puppet show - juggle - rap - be a ventriloquist - do a short dramatic scene - dance; hip-hop, ballet, tap, jazz, swing, ethnic... play a musical instrument - be a comedian; tell jokes, riddles, do a funny monologue, a short sketch - recite poetry - impersonate a famous person - dress up like a super hero or magic wizard...

Please prepare an act that is two minutes in length or less.

- -

PRODUCTION SESSIONS:

AUDITION	MONDAY	MARCH 18	
REHEARSAL	TUESDAY	MARCH 26	*(8 days after audition)*
REHEARSAL	WEDNESDAY	MARCH 27	

PERFORMANCES:

7 PM	WEDNESDAY	MARCH 27	TICKETS: ADULTS CHILDREN	$5.00 $2.50
MORNING ASSEMBLY	THURSDAY	MARCH 28	*Lower grades* *Free admission*	
7 PM	THURSDAY	MARCH 28	TICKETS: ADULTS CHILDREN	$5.00 $2.50
MORNING ASSEMBLY	FRIDAY	MARCH 29	*Upper grades* *Free admission*	

STEP 2: SIGN UP YOUR PERFORMERS

FORM #2—THE SIGN-UP SHEET

Name the form: *Talent Show Sign-Up Sheet*
Include the name of your show: _____
Request performer information: *(See sample "Talent Show Sign-up Sheet" form).*
Provide space for parent or guardian's signature
List conditions
Provide space for the director's notations.

STEP 3: SIGN UP YOUR CREW & MC CANDIDATES

FORM #3—REQUEST FOR CREW & MC CANDIDATES:

Name the form: *Request for Crew & MC Candidates*
Include the name of your show: _____
Address your request to specific people:
    Teachers
    Youth group leaders…
Specify the number of people needed (total of 12):
    1 Stage manager
    3 Green-room supervisors
    1 Curtain operator
    2 Follow-spotlight operators
    5 MC candidates
Provide space for your stage crew and MC candidates to sign their names. *(See sample form).*

SAMPLE SIGN-UP SHEET

The Sign-up Sheet is printed on the reverse side of the Talent Show Announcement

THE ROGERS REVUE

Name: *Jimmy Cruz* Age: *10* Grade: *4* Home phone: *(555) 234-5678* Home room teacher: *Mr. Beck* Rm. *11*

Describe your act - what you plan to do: *Ventriloquism* Name of your act (only if there are three or more people in it):

N/A _____

First and last names of everyone in your act: *Jimmy Cruz* _____

(Groups: List names on separate page - Please staple name list and sign-up sheets together).

Who taught/coached/helped you with your act: *Cynthia Cruz* Relationship: *Aunt* _____

Name of your accompanist: *N/A* _____ Name of Song: *N/A* _____

Performing experience: *The American Legion* Who or what gave you the idea for your act: *Aunt Cynthia*

Who is your favorite famous person *Jim Carrey*

   ▸▸   Alternate choice: _____ COMEDY: *Yes*   COSTUME PARADE? *No*

I GIVE MY CHILD *Jimmy Cruz* _____ PERMISSION TO PARTICIPATE IN THE ROGERS REVUE

SIGNATURE: *Fernando Cruz* _____ RELATIONSHIP: *Father* DATE: *3/12/2003*

CONDITIONS:

    1. Please prepare an act that is two minutes in length or less

    2. Participants must attend all three production sessions: The audition and both rehearsals.

    3. At rehearsals or whenever live accompanists are not available, cassette tapes will be used. If you or your child plan to use musical accompaniment, we ask that it be recorded on, or transferred to, cassette tape.

       (If you need help with this, our sound technician will assist you.)

    4. Remember to bring your performing equipment to the audition. Eg. Dancing shoes, musical instruments, music, props, tapes…

    5. Words to songs, poems and comedy material must be written out or photocopied and stapled to your sign-up sheet. If the director feels that material is objectionable (obscene, sacrilegious, violent or insulting) performers will be recast. (See alternate choice, above).

    6. Participants may be grouped with other acts, if more than 30 acts audition.

    7. If you are under 18 years of age, sign-up sheets must be signed and dated by a parent or guardian.

    8. Please return your completed sign-up sheet to the school office by *March 14*.

- -*Please do not write below this line)*- -

THE DIRECTOR'S NOTATIONS:

Name of act:_____   Type of Act:_____

Tune_____   Key: _____

       Tempo: _____

Accompanist:_____   Tape: _____

Start:_____   Finish_____ Time:_____

Number of people:_____Space needed: _____   Props: _____

Microphone:_____Alternate choice:_____   Placement code____ ____ ____Total:_____

SAMPLE REQUEST FOR CREW AND MC CANDIDATES FORM

THE ROGERS REVUE

TO: FIFTH GRADE TEACHERS - *Please Return this form to the school office by:* **March 14**

Mr. Ramon Gutierrez   Classroom 17
Ms. Eve Jefferson   Classroom 18
Ms. Elvira Reiner   Classroom 19

Please get together with your fellow 5th grade teachers, listed above, and recommend students suitable for, and interested in being members of the crew or MC candidates.

A total of twelve students are needed.

One stage manager
One curtain operator
Two follow-spotlight operators
Three green-room supervisors
Five MC candidates

The MC will be reading the introductions - no need to memorize.
The crew and the MC candidates may also be in an act.
The MC candidates are invited to join the comedy team.
All participants must fill out a sign-up sheet and have a parent or guardian sign and date it.
It is understood that these students will keep up with, or make up, missed school work.

Stage manager:	*Frankie Bahar*	Classroom	19
Curtain operator:	*Dora Cummings*	Classroom	18
Follow-spotlight operator:	*Kim Lee*	Classroom	17
Follow-spotlight operator:	*Rumi Sharif*	Classroom	18
Green-room supervisor:	*Sheeba O'Connor*	Classroom	17
Green-room supervisor:	*Latania Lincoln*	Classroom	18
Green-room supervisor:	*Vanessa Cruz*	Classroom	19
MC candidate:	*Freddie Wong*	Classroom	17
MC candidate:	*John Paris*	Classroom	17
MC candidate:	*Yolanda Gillette*	Classroom	18
MC candidate:	*Jose Salazar*	Classroom	19
MC candidate:	*Hezakiah Jones*	Classroom	19

SCHOOL SHOWS—REQUEST A STAFF LIST AND A SCHOOL SCHEDULE:

Ask the school secretary for a staff list that includes the names of:
The school office staff
Teachers and their classroom numbers
Day custodian
Night custodian
A lunch, recess and dismissal schedule.

REQUEST ASSISTANCE FROM THE CUSTODIAN—ALL SHOWS:

Meet with the custodian and ask to see the location of:
1.   Follow-spotlight outlet (220 Volts) at the rear of the performance site.
2.   Curtain control/rope pulley (if there is a front curtain).
3.   Backstage house lights' switch.
4.   Lighting control panel:
          Peripheral auditorium lighting options
          Stage lighting options.
5.   Check to see if the stage and the entrances to the stage are free of clutter. If they aren't, request a clear stage and clear entrances.
6.   Ask to be shown how to set-up and use the in-house sound system.
7.   If the in-house sound system doesn't have a cassette player already connected to it, ask to be shown how to patch into the system with an imported player.
8.   Check to see if the light switches are clearly marked. If they aren't, identify each switch. (We suggest small pieces of masking tape marked with a fine-point marker.)
9.   Find the switches that de-activate the electrical outlets and mark them *don't touch!"*

THE FIVE CATEGORIES OF ACTS:

Upon receiving the filled-in sign-up sheets from the coordinator, the director separates them into the following five categories:
1.   MOVEMENT/DANCE
2.   COMEDY
3.   VOCAL
4.   INSTRUMENTAL
5.   NOVELTY (Anything other than movement/dance, comedy, vocal or instrumental goes into the novelty category. For example: Magic, juggling, baton twirling…).

SAMPLE SIGN-UP SUMMARY—THE ROGERS REVUE:

For the purpose of clarification, let's suppose that the following acts have signed up to participate in *The Rogers Revue*:

Movement/Dance Category	*No. of people*	*Grades*
Break-dance	3	3/5
Russian folk	2	3/5
Chinese Ribbon	3	5
Ballet	1	4
Tahitian	1	3
Swing (whole class)	30	5
Hip-Hop	6	4
Gymnastics	6	4
Fifties	7	Teachers
Total: 9 *Acts*	*59 Performers*	

Comedy category:		
Sketch	2	3/5
Jokes—MC Understudy	1	5
Riddles—MC Candidate	1	5
Jokes—MC Candidate	1	5
Jokes—MC Candidate	1	5
Total: 5 *Acts*	*6 Performers*	

Vocal category:		
Country	2	4
Irish ballad	1	2
French ballad	1	3
Rhythm & Blues	1	5
Standard	1	Kindergarten
Total: 5 *Acts*	*6 Performers*	

Instrumental category:	*No. of People*	*Grades*
Flute—Classical	1	5
Trumpet—Jazz	1	5
Total: *2 Acts*	*2 Performers*	

Novelty category:

Impersonator	1	3
Ventriloquist	1	4
Baton-twirler	1	5
Mime	1	4

Total: *4 Acts* ⠀⠀⠀⠀⠀⠀⠀⠀⠀*4 Performers*

<u>GRAND TOTAL—</u>
⠀⠀⠀*25* ACTS ⠀⠀⠀⠀⠀⠀⠀⠀⠀⠀⠀*77* PERFORMERS

<u>FINDING HELP—SIGN-UP SHEET DISCOVERIES:</u>

A wealth of information can be found on the filled-in sign-up sheets.
For example:
⠀⠀Choreographers
⠀⠀Accompanists
⠀⠀Comedy coaches
⠀⠀Music teachers
⠀⠀Voice and drama coaches
⠀⠀Dance teachers…

The following is a sampling of the kinds of responses that can usually be found on the sign-up sheets, in answer to the question:

"Who taught/coached/helped you with your act?"
⠀⠀Vocalist—Jenny Zimmer ⠀⠀ Morning Kindergarten
⠀⠀***Vocal coach/accompanist***: ⠀⠀ *Aunt—Goldie Zimmer/Pianist*

⠀⠀Trumpet Player—Eileen O'Connor ⠀ Grade 5
⠀⠀***Music teacher***: ⠀⠀ *William Marasco*

⠀⠀Rapper—Tyrone Brown and the ⠀⠀ Grade 5
⠀⠀West Side Hip-Hop Crew
⠀⠀***Choreographer***: ⠀⠀ *Mom—Tyra Washington*
⠀⠀⠀⠀⠀⠀⠀⠀⠀⠀⠀⠀⠀⠀⠀ *PTA President*

⠀⠀Dancer—Jenny Rudenko ⠀⠀ Grade 3
⠀⠀Dancer—Dimitri Rudenko ⠀⠀ Grade 5
⠀⠀***Dance coach/accompanist***: ⠀⠀ *Mom—Gigi Rudenko/Drums*

Comedienne—Mandy Epstein	Grade 3
Comedian—Joey Epstein	Grade 5
Comedy coach:	*Grandfather—Nat Epstein*
Impersonator—Arnie Prince	Grade 3
Elvis coach:	*Dad—Alex Prince*
Mime—Florence Jordan	Grade 4
Mime coach:	*Mom—Jeanette Jordan*

The sign-up sheets help you to discover helpful people with specific interests, who can be called on for assistance.

SAMPLE ALL-PURPOSE SHOW—CELEBRATING CLARKSVILLE:
An announcement/sign-up sheet is given to:
    Members of the school safety patrol (11 and 12 year-olds)
    Law enforcement personnel and their families.

FINDING YOUR CREW—ADDITIONAL OPTIONS:
If by audition time, your crew positions have not been filled, consider asking the parents and/or friends of your performers to help out.

ALERTING THE MEDIA:
About a month before the performance dates, you may want to contact:
    Local newspaper offices
    Radio stations
    Television stations

After finding out who the community events' contact people are, mail, fax or e-mail press releases to each of them.

FORM #4—THE PRESS RELEASE:

Name the form:	Press Release
Mention your producer or sponsoring organization	_____
Include the name of your show	_____
Indicate who your performers will be	_____
List performance site	_____
List performance dates and times	_____

List ticket sales contact person and phone number   _____
List ticket price   _____
Mention fund raising recipient   _____

SAMPLE PRESS RELEASE:

The Clarksville Police Department Proudly Presents
A Spectacular Talent Show!

CELEBRATING CLARKSVILLE

Starring: Police Personnel, Safety Patrol Students and Mystery Guest Artists

PERFORMANCES WILL TAKE PLACE AT THE CLARKSVILLE GYMNASIUM

FRIDAY	MAY 24th	7 PM
SATURDAY	MAY 25th	7 PM
SUNDAY	MAY 26th	2 PM

Ticket Sales: Officer Rodney Vierra (555) 555-0015
ADULTS $10   CHILDREN $5

Proceeds will be contributed to the Boys & Girls Club of Clarksville

TOO FEW ACTS HAVE SIGNED UP TO BE IN YOUR SHOW?

Let's suppose that after reviewing the overall turnout you decide that:
     Not enough acts have signed up to be in your show
     Not enough acts have signed up in a particular category.

Solution #1:

Meet with the people at your church, school, corporation, etc. and give them a pep talk.

Inquire: Who has a special skill? (Often one person will speak up for another).
     Dance?
     Sing?
     Tell jokes?
     Do voices/impersonations?

Play a musical instrument?
Yo-yo tricks?
Twirl a hula hoop?

Hand out sign-up sheets and recruit performers on the spot.

Solution #2—INVITE GUEST ARTISTS:

You may want to consider contacting one or more of the various creative and performing arts teachers in your community. They are usually grateful for the opportunity to showcase their students.
Dance Studios
Vocal and Drama Coaches
Music Teachers…

Ask for help and recommendations from:
Your Local Magic Store
Comedy Club
Martial Arts Studio…

TOO MANY ACTS HAVE SIGNED UP TO BE IN YOUR SHOW?

Let's suppose that after reviewing the sign-up sheets, you find that the overall turnout is enormous.

Solution #1:

Confer with your producer and show coordinator to consider forming two completely separate shows.
For example:
"Celebrating Clarksville—The Red Unit"
"Celebrating Clarksville—The Blue Unit"

One show could be presented during the current month and one show could be presented the following month.

Solution #2:

Be on the alert (at the audition) for movement or dance acts that are similar in style and combine them.

Novelty acts that are of the same sort, like martial arts demonstrators (for instance) could perform one after the other in the same act.

Line them up according to their relative skill level:

Beginner	First
Intermediate	Next
Advanced	Last

Solution #3:

Observe which acts have obviously put very little time and effort into preparing. Consider their *alternate choice* preference and invite them to participate accordingly (in either the costume parade or a comedy sketch).

GUEST ARTISTS
If after counting the sign-up sheets, you find that not enough people
have signed up to be in your show,
you may want to consider contacting one or more of the various
performing arts teachers in your community
They are usually grateful for the opportunity to showcase their students.

SHOW COORDINATOR'S CHECK LIST

NAME OF SHOW: _____

AUDITION LOCATION: _____Date: _____Time: _____

REHEARSAL/PERFORMANCE LOCATION: _____ _____

1st REHEARSAL: Date: _____Time: _____

2nd REHEARSAL: Date: _____Time: _____

1st PERFORMANCE   Date: _____Time: _____

2nd PERFORMANCE: Date: _____Time: _____

3rd PERFORMANCE: Date: _____Time: _____

TICKET PRICE: Adults: $_____Children $_____

NUMBER OF SEATS/TICKETS AVAILABLE FOR EACH PERFORMANCE: _____

PRINT AND DISTRIBUTE ANNOUNCEMENT/SIGN-UP SHEETS: Date: _____

PRINT AND DISTRIBUTE CREW/MC CANDIDATE FORM: Date: _____

PICK UP SIGN-UP SHEETS & CREW MC CANDIDATE FORM: Date: _____

PRINT TICKETS: Date: _____

PRINT PROGRAMS: Date: _____

ACCOUTREMENTS:

- ☐ Sound system
- ☐ Stage
- ☐ Stage lighting
- ☐ Follow-spotlight and spare bulb
- ☐ Platform for follow-spotlight
- ☐ Backdrop and wings
- ☐ Audience seating: Sloped or flat? _____   Folding chairs or fixed seating? _____
- ☐ Stairs for finale parade
- ☐ Green-room seating   Folding chairs or benches?   _____
- ☐ Two tables—One 6' long and one any size

VOLUNTEERS:

- ☐ Ticket sales   Tickets and table for ticket sales
- ☐ Video camera operator   Video camera, tripod and videotapes
- ☐ Photographer   Camera and film
- ☐ Refreshment sales   Refreshments and table
- ☐ Souvenir sales   Souvenirs and table
- ☐ Ushers   Programs for ushers to distribute
- ☐ Security

SAMPLE SIGN UP SUMMARY—CELEBRATING CLARKSVILLE:

Movement/Dance category:

Tap	1 person	Guest artist	Age 16
Igorot tribal	3 people	Officer's family	Age 9
Rope skippers	5 people	Safety patrol	Age 11
Hip-hop	6 people	Guest artists	Ages 16-18
Can Can	6 people	Guest artists	Ages 16-18
Irish clog	10 people	Guest artists	Ages 16-18
Flamenco	10 people	Guest artists	Adult
TOTAL: 7 ACTS	*41 PERFORMERS*		

Comedy category:

Stand-up	2 people	Safety patrol	Age 11
Stand-up	1 person	Safety patrol	Age 11
Stand-up	1 person	Safety patrol	Age 11
Stand-up	1 person	Safety patrol	Age 11
Stand-up	1 person	Officer's son	Age 9
Monologue	1 person	Officer/MC	Adult
TOTAL: 6 ACTS	*7 PERFORMERS*		

Vocal category:

Patriotic	1 person	Safety patrol	Age 11
Country	3 people	Officer/twin sons	Adult/Age 7
Hawaiian	1 person	Safety patrol	Age 11
R & B	3 people	Guest artists	Ages 16-17
Standard	1 person	Officer's daughter	Age 5
Top-40	1 person	Safety patrol	Age 11
TOTAL: 6 ACTS	*10 PERFORMERS*		

Instrumental category:

Tuba	1 person	Police Officer	Adult
Harmonica	1 person	Safety Patrol	Age 11
Fiddle	1 person	Police Officer	Adult
TOTAL: 3 ACTS	*3 PERFORMERS*		

Novelty category:

Color guard	4 people	Safety Patrol	Age 11
Cheerleaders	10 people	Guest Artists	Age 16-18
Magician	1 person	Police Officer	Adult
Juggler	1 person	Police Officer	Adult
Fashion show	12 people	Guest Artists	Ages 16-18
TOTAL: 5 ACTS	*28 PERFORMERS*		

GRAND TOTAL—SAMPLE SHOW—"CELEBRATING CLARKSVILLE"

27 ACTS   89 PERFORMERS

CHAPTER SEVEN

THE AUDITION

The director and the sound technician arrive at the audition site about an hour before the audition is scheduled to begin.

THE DIRECTOR'S OBJECTIVES:

Create an atmosphere of encouragement and approval
Conduct MC try-outs
Establish a strong beginning for each act
Make sure that each act is the correct length
Establish a definite ending for each act.

THE DIRECTOR'S SUPPLIES—AUDITION AND/OR REHEARSALS:

A stopwatch (for timing acts)
Four clipboards (one for the director, and one for each of the three green-room supervisors)
Stapler
Plenty of sharpened pencils with erasers
Notepaper
Blue painter's masking tape (for marking performance boundaries)
Yardstick
String (for surveying sight lines)
Yellow felt-tipped highlighter (for marking technical worksheets)
Black construction paper (for backing the MC's cue sheet)
Kitchen timer (for limiting time spent rehearsing individual acts)
Video camera, tripod and plenty of blank videotapes.

THE SOUND TECHNICIAN'S SUPPLIES—AUDITION AND/OR REHEARSALS:

Extension cord
Portable cassette/CD player
An extra cassette deck with headphones

Blank cassette tapes (at least 10)
A cassette tray (for keeping tapes organized)
Graphic correction tape (for labeling cassettes)
A fine-point permanent marker (for marking cassettes).

SETTING UP FOR THE AUDITION—ALL SHOWS:

The sound system and follow-spotlight are not needed at the audition.

1. Table #1 and two chairs.
    A six-foot long table (for the director and sound technician's use) is positioned in the middle of the audience space, about eight feet back from the front edge of the stage or performing area.
    The right half of the table is used as a writing surface by the director.
    The left half of the table is used by the sound technician for a portable cassette/CD player
    Two chairs are positioned at this table, facing the performing area.
2. Table #2 (any size) is placed near the entrance to the performance site.
    For school shows the sign-up sheets are stacked on this table, according to grade. For all other shows, the sign-up sheets are stacked alphabetically, according to the name of the act.
3. A piano or electronic keyboard is positioned near the stage, off to the side (so it doesn't obstruct the director's view).
4. The front curtain, if there is one, remains open.
5. The house lights stay on.
6. Chairs or benches (for about thirty performers) are set up along the right side wall, near the performing area.
7. A video camera is set up. (The fairly complicated step of lining up the show can be made *considerably* easier if the audition is videotaped.
    The director uses the videotape later for reviewing purposes, when preparing for the first rehearsal).

GREEN-ROOM SUPERVISORS—ALL SHOWS:

The green-room supervisors assist the director by organizing performers. They are asked to:
    Greet performers as they arrive at the audition site.
    Give each act or act leader their sign-up sheet(s) to hold until it's their turn to audition.

Ask performers, who have signed up to audition, to be seated on the chairs or benches that were set up in the green-room area.

Assist performers (especially the younger ones) so that they will be *completely* ready when the director asks them to audition.

For example:

Dancing shoes:	Should be on the dancer's feet
Musical instruments:	Should be out of their cases, assembled and in the musician's hand
Props:	Should be unpacked and ready
Cassette tapes:	Should be cued up. (An extra tape deck with headphones, is provided for this purpose).

ESTABLISH A CLUTTER-FREE GREEN-ROOM RIGHT FROM THE START:

We suggest that you designate a separate area where all extra things (backpacks, sweaters, jackets, etc.) can be stored while performers are auditioning.

ORDER OF THE AUDITION—SCHOOL SHOWS:

1. As soon as possible, after attendance has been taken, the fifth grade teachers (or whichever grade is highest in the school) are asked to send the crew and the MC candidates to the auditorium.
2. The director gives each of the MC candidates a sample cue sheet to look at for a few minutes while he or she meets the crew and gives them a brief description of their jobs.
3. If any of the stage crew signed up to perform, they audition at this time.
4. The green-room supervisors are asked to stay and help the director.
5. All other crew members are sent back to class.

When instructed to do so by the director, the green-room supervisors bring performers from their classrooms to the auditorium.

Before going to the auditorium, each student is asked whether or not they have their performing equipment with them. If they have forgotten it, they cannot audition at this time. For the time being these particular students remain in their classrooms.

FORGOTTEN EQUIPMENT:

Auditioning students who forgot their dancing shoes, cassette tapes, props, music, musical instruments, etc.

Possible solutions:

1.   Have someone from home bring the forgotten equipment to school. The director could audition these students later in the day when their performing equipment arrives.
2.   Arrange to have the director audition these students later that evening when a parent or guardian is available to bring the child and their performing equipment back to the audition site.

STEP 4: HOLD MC TRY-OUTS

The director explains to the MC candidates that the cues (written in capital letters and underlined) are trigger phrases that set many things in motion.
For example:
1.   An act's music begins (for those who use music).
2.   The curtain opens (for acts that use the full stage).
3.   The follow-spotlight moves from the MC, who has just spoken the cue, to the performer who is entering.
4.   Applause begins.

The director demonstrates the difference between poor delivery and effective delivery:

A monotone speech pattern	A well-modulated voice
Mumbling	Clear diction
A lackluster greeting	An enthusiastic welcome.

The MC candidates are told that they will be graded on the following:
Reading ability
Clarity of diction
Energy
Enthusiasm
Friendliness.

THREE SAMPLE CUES:

Without using a microphone, each MC candidate in succession, is asked to stand about six feet away from the director and read three cues. They are asked to:
Pay particular attention to punctuation
Pause and breathe whenever they see a period
Pause longer and take a very deep breath whenever they see a dash.

Sample Cue #1:

At Allen School in Bonita they always start their shows off in a big way, with a line of dancers. Three years ago, they did the Cancan. Two years ago, they did the Charleston. This year, they are doing a tap routine from a Broadway show. Maxine Clark and Sue Phelps choreographed their routine. Their costumes are by Peggy Foster and their make-up by Charlene Fox.
Look out for—THE ALLEN SCHOOL TOPPERS!

Sample Cue #2:

Our next act has been studying music with Jim Gates for the past two years. He has performed for his class and at Sunday school. His favorite performer is Johnny Cash…Here now to play his guitar and sing for us is—
Our Master of Ceremonies—ERIC MASON!

Sample Cue #3:

And now, a multi-talented performer—
Here's Chula Vista's Own—MARIO LOPEZ!

The director jots down a separate rating of one to five (five being the best) in each of three categories, for each of the MC candidates:

(1-5)	Reading ability
(1-5)	Clarity of diction
(1-5)	Energy/Enthusiasm

MC CANDIDATE RATINGS—Sample Show—The Rogers Revue:

The candidate with the highest rating will be the MC
The candidate with the next highest rating will be the Understudy:

Candidate	Reading Ability	Clarity of Diction	Energy/Enthusiasm	Total
J. Salazar	4	3	3	10
J. Paris	3	2	3	8
Y. Gillette	4	4	5	13
F. Wong	3	4	3	10
H. Jones	5	5	5	15

If any of the candidates signed up to perform, they are auditioned at this time. All five candidates are invited to join the comedy team.

The MC candidates are asked to meet with the comedy coach at an appointed time.

YOUR COMEDY COACH:

Instead of delegating this job, your director may choose to be the comedy coach him or herself. Otherwise, your comedy coach could be:
1.   Someone who is listed as a comedy coach for one of the acts on a sign-up sheet (and the material that was submitted is very amusing).
2.   A boy/girl scout leader or a recreation counselor who is experienced in directing comedy skits for after-school programs, summer camp...

AUDITIONING PERFORMERS BY GRADE:

By now your first group of performers has arrived from their classrooms and is ready to audition. Group One includes:
Morning kindergarten (morning kindergarten students are always seen first because of early dismissal)
Grades 1, 2, and 3.
If any of these acts have partners in the upper grades, they are sent for (so that they can audition with their lower-grade partners).

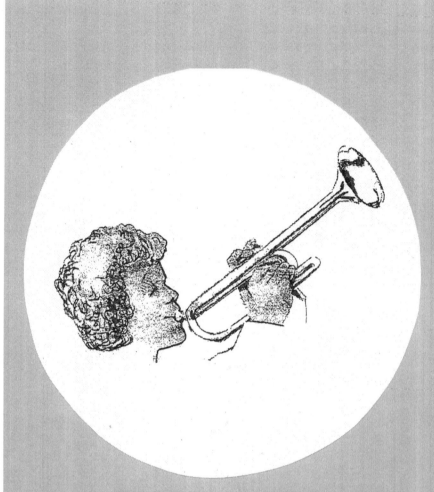

MUSICAL ACTS/INSTRUMENTALISTS
Young musicians often choose music that is too difficult for them.
They slow down on the more demanding passages and speed up
on the easier ones, causing their listeners to feel uncomfortable.
It is essential that instrumentalists choose a song that they can play
without hesitation.

Sample Group One—The Rogers Revue:

Please note: Within each group, the acts with the most performers in them are seen first (*with the exception of morning kindergarten*) so that more students can be sent back to class sooner.

Morning kindergarten	*1*	*Vocalist*
Grade 3/5	3	Break dancers
Grade 3/5	2	Russian folk dancers
Grade 3/5	2	Comedians
Grade 2	1	Vocalist
Grade 3	1	Tahitian dancer
Grade 3	1	Vocalist
Grade 3	1	Elvis impersonator
	12 Performers	*8 Acts*

After the director has auditioned the *second act* in the first group, two of the green-room supervisors are asked to bring the next group to the auditorium and help them to get ready.

The third green-room supervisor stays in the auditorium and assists by sending the next act to the director when he or she is ready to audition them. *The objective is to keep the auditioning process moving forward, without delays.*

Sample Group Two—The Rogers Revue:

Grade 5 (Whole class)	30	Swing dancers
Grade 4	6	Gymnasts
Grade 4	2	Vocalists
Grade 4	1	Ventriloquist
Grade 4	1	Ballet dancer
Grade 4	1	Mime
	41 Performers	*6 Acts*

Sample Group Three—The Rogers Revue:

Grade 5	6	Hip-hop dancers
Grade 5	3	Chinese ribbon dancers
Grade 5	1	Vocalist
Grade 5	1	Trumpet player
Grade 5	1	Flute player
Grade 5	1	Baton twirler
	13 Performers	*6 Acts*

Performing teachers—The Rogers Revue:
The hypothetical seven teachers who signed up to dance to a 50's tune are asked to come to the auditorium after school to show the director their routine.

COMEDY COACH MEETING:

A suggested comedy meeting format:
1. The comedy coach demonstrates various (age appropriate) comedy sketches to the comedy team (MC candidates and alternate choice acts).
2. Each student is asked which "bit" they would most like to be in, and if they prefer to be the straight man (see glossary) or play the comedic role.
3. Each student is asked to say a couple of lines in character, for whatever joke or comedy sketch is being discussed at the moment.
4. The comedy coach starts with the funniest material and casts the comics with the best delivery first.
5. Comedy team members are asked to tell a joke or riddle to the group (if they care to). The comedy coach will probably add this material to the show if the jokes are funny and non-offensive.
6. The comedy coach makes sure that everyone on the team is cast and makes a list of who was cast, and in which comedy segment.
7. The comedy team members are given scripts and asked to learn their lines, so that they will be ready in time for the first rehearsal.

WHERE TO FIND IDEAS FOR COMEDY MATERIAL:

Your public library
The Internet (books on comedy writing, skits/sketches, joke files…)

TIMING MUSICAL INTRODUCTIONS:

The director times each act's introduction with a stopwatch.

Most amateur performers allow way too much time to elapse before beginning their routines.

On a medium-sized stage, a four bar intro (about six seconds) is usually plenty of time to get from the wings to center stage, or wherever the starting position for an act happens to be.

Counting beats and bars:

In 4/4 tempo (four beats to the bar) the count for a four bar introduction would be:

    (1)-2-3-4,   *(2)-2-3-4,*   *(3)-2-3-4,*   *(4)-2-3-4.*

STEP 5: AUDITIONING PERFORMERS

A SAMPLE AUDITION:

The first performer to be seen by the director at our sample audition is kinder-garten student, five-year-old Jenny Zimmer.

For the purpose of illustration, let's suppose that Jenny brought a note with her that states that her Aunt Goldie recorded her piano accompaniment onto a cassette tape for Jenny to sing along with at the audition, rehearsals and assemblies. At the evening performances Aunt Goldie will play for her in person.

1. The director asks Jenny for her sign-up sheet and walks with her to the stage.
2. The sound technician is given her cassette tape and Jenny is asked if she is ready to begin.
3. The director times her musical introduction with a stopwatch and notes its length.
4. While Jenny is singing she receives the director's approving, complete, undivided attention.
5. When Jenny has finished singing, the director applauds and encourages everyone in the auditorium to applaud too.
6. The director makes a note of the song's length.
7. The director fills out the *Director's Notations* portion of Jenny's sign-up sheet and explains to her that her musical introduction will be shortened.
8. So she can hear exactly how it will sound, the sound technician plays Jenny's tape, using the last four bars of her intro.
9. Jenny begins her song at the new place with no problem. This reinforces to the director that Jenny has understood.
10. Items pertaining to Jenny's act are stapled together and placed under the clip on the director's clipboard:
    Her sign-up sheet
    The lyrics to her song
    The note from Aunt Goldie
11. The director praises Jenny for doing well at her audition.

12. One of the green-room supervisors walks with Jenny and sees her safely back to her kindergarten classroom.

THE DIRECTOR'S NOTATIONS:

The notations on Jenny's sign-up sheet would look like this:

Name of Act: *Jenny Zimmer*   Type of Act: *Vocal (Standard)*
Tune: *Over the Rainbow*   Key: *F*   Tempo: *Slow*
Accompanist: *Aunt Goldie Zimmer-Piano (Performances)*   Tape: *(Rehearsals)*
Start: *4 Bar Intro.* Finish: *After 1 ½ Choruses. (Variation/Circus bow)*   Time: *1:15*
Number of people: *1*   Space needed: *In One* Props: *None*
Microphone: *HHM*   Alternate choice: *CP*   Placement: *5 5 4*   Total: *14*

EXPLANATION OF THE DIRECTOR'S NOTATIONS:
NAMING ACTS:

Single acts:
If there is only one person in an act, we feel it is best to use their real name, unless of course they have their heart set on choosing a stage name. In the above sample the child's name is Jenny Zimmer and the name of the act is *Jenny Zimmer.*

Double acts:
When there are two people in an act, they are sometimes referred to as a double act or duo. Using last names can give a theatrical ring to an act's name.
For example:
> Wegner & Stutzman
> Lane & McCardy

If there are three or more people in an act:
Ask your performers to think up an interesting sounding name.
For instance:
> Tyrone Brown and the West Side Hip-Hop Crew
> The Surfin' Sensations

TYPE OF ACT:

In the "director's notations" section of the sign-up sheet, whatever category the act fits into followed by *a more specific description,* would be written on that particular line. For example:
> Movement/Dance   *Gymnastics...*
> Comedy   *Monologue...*

Vocal	*Standard...*
Instrumental	*Saxophone...*
Novelty	*Impersonator...*

TUNE:

If an act plays a musical instrument or sings, or if they use any type of background music whatsoever, the name of the song that is used in their act would be written after the word, *"tune"*.

KEY:

If an act uses live musical accompaniment, and their music must be played in a particular key (because they sing or play a musical instrument, for instance) that information is written after the word, *"key"*.

TEMPO:

The speed at which an act's (live) music should be played is noted.

ACCOMPANIST:

The name and relationship of the accompanist to the performer and the musical instrument that the accompanist plays, is listed after the word, *"accompanist"*.

Aunt	Goldie Zimmer	Piano
Uncle	Francois Lumet	Accordion
Mom	Gigi Rudenko	Percussion

TAPE:

If an act uses recorded music at performances and/or rehearsals, that information is indicated after the word, *"tape"*.

At rehearsals

At rehearsals and performances.

START:

How an act begins is noted.

Make it possible for your performers to start their routines without delay. It is very important to treat the audience with the utmost respect and not keep them waiting.

Please refer to *"timing musical introductions"* listed earlier in this chapter, which states, *"a four bar introduction is usually plenty of time for performers to get from the wings to center stage"*.

Make sure that your performers understand how much of their music is being deleted so that they can be confident about when to start singing, dancing, etc.

PRECISION CUEING:

When a cassette tape is properly cued-up, that is, rewound to a point just before the onset of the desired sound, a performer's music can be started precisely.
Directions:
1.   Press the play button on your tape recorder and listen for the *"attack"* sound of the desired music. *Stop as soon as you here the attack (See glossary).*
2.   Remove the cassette from the player.
3.   Holding the cassette in your right hand with the exposed tape opening toward you, place your left little finger (or a pencil) in the left hole.
4.   *Turn the left reel a quarter-turn clockwise.* Doing this rewinds the tape to a point just before the attack. Practice this a few times until the desired result (of having the music start instantaneously) is achieved.

Acts who work without musical accompaniment such as:
   Mimes
   Martial arts demonstrators
   Comedians
   Poets
   Dramatic actors
   Some magicians…

These acts are instructed by the director to:
   Get into position on stage as quickly as possible
   Start their routine without delay.

FINISH—HOW EACH ACT ENDS IS NOTED:

The director helps each act decide exactly how their act will end:
1.   *A visual cue:*
      A bow
      Pose
      Gesture
      Wave…

2.   *A spoken cue:*
       "Thank you"
       "You've been a great audience"
3.   *A musical cue*—Acts who use music will either finish: At a particular place in the music. (At the end of a chorus, for example)
       Or, their ending will be a *fade-out* ending.
       The phrase (in the lyrics) just before the fade-out is noted.
       Or, the musical treatment just before the fade-out is indicated.
       For instance: After the guitar solo.

TIME:

The precise length of each act is noted.

NUMBER OF PEOPLE

The number of people in each act is noted.

SPACE NEEDED: *(This notation is omitted if there is no front curtain).*

   In one (the area that is in front of the closed, front curtain).
   Performers who don't require very much space use this area: Singers, stand-up comedians, instrumentalists…

   Full stage—Acts who truly need more space, such as: Gymnasts, most dancers…(If there were a front curtain, it would open for these acts.)

PROPS:

If an act uses a prop, that information is documented. For example:
   Magician's table
   Artist's easel
   Music stand
   Gymnastic mats (3)
   Chairs (2)…

MICROPHONE:

If an act uses a microphone, the type of set-up required is noted:
   HHM: Hand held microphone
   M/S: Microphone on a microphone-stand
   M/P: Microphone on a pillow (to amplify floor sounds)

ALTERNATE CHOICE:

In the event that the director finds it necessary to recast an act, each performer's alternate choice is documented:

Costume parade

Comedy

PLACEMENT:

When deciding where to place an act on the show, there are three main considerations.

Effort in preparing:

Rating 1-5	One:	Unprepared
	Five:	Very well prepared

Strengths:

Rating 1-5	One:	Poor rhythm (for example)
	Five:	Excellent rhythm

Charisma

Rating 1-5	One:	Monotonous, mechanical, low energy
	Five:	A strong, heartfelt, connection to the audience.

The placement code is strictly confidential and for the director's eyes only!

INFLUENCING FACTORS:

Factors to consider when rating acts in the various categories:

Dance/Movement:	Rhythm
	Agility.
Comedians:	Well-written, funny material
	Good timing and delivery.
Vocalists:	Intonation (accuracy of musical pitch)
	Rhythm.
Instrumentalists:	Intonation
	Rhythm.
Novelty acts:	Innovation
	Proficiency.

TIMING ACTS:

There is an age-old axiom in show business that states:
"Always leave 'em wanting more!"

It is the director's job to decide what the best length for each act is. Time given to an act depends on what is being done and whether or not they are holding the audiences' interest and attention.

There is a point at which the audience is eagerly listening and enjoying what is being presented. Seconds later, the performance has gone beyond that elusive point and the observer begins to wonder, *"When is this going to end?"*

The director should be aware of his or her gut feeling. By ending an act before interest wanes, even the most inexperienced performer can sparkle.

If there are fewer acts in your show, don't try to s-t-r-e-t-c-h by allowing each act to have more time. *Simply have a shorter show.*

FOCUS:

Performers, who are on stage, but not being featured at the moment, should look at the one who is. It directs the audience's attention and gives the performer, who is currently in the background, something theatrical to do.

DANCERS:

As soon as a dancer has entered, a good way to start a routine is with a pose, either with their back toward the audience or facing front.

Dancers are advised to:
1. Practice looking at the audience and at each other with friendly glances, rather than at their feet, or the floor.
2. Practice in front of a mirror at home, so they can see for themselves how good it looks when they are evenly spaced.
3. The ones who know the routine the best, should be in front and in the center.

MUSIC FOR NOVELTY ACTS
When choosing musical accompaniment for your novelty acts, *think variety!*
Try contrasting the music of your dancers,
vocalists and instrumentalists with something entirely different;
perhaps Asian, African, Middle-Eastern or Salsa sounds

Silence can also provide a strong contrast.
The guttural and other intense sounds made by martial arts demonstrators
can be more distinctly heard when there is no musical accompaniment at all.

VOCALISTS:

1.   Vocalists sound best when they are singing within their range. Some songs have a much wider range than others. For instance, our national anthem; some notes are very high and some are very low.
2.   Singers should also be sure that the song that they have chosen to sing is in the correct key for them. A song can easily be transposed if it is too high or too low. Most choir directors and accompanists can help vocalists find their best key.

INSTRUMENTALISTS:

Young musicians often choose music that is too difficult for them. They slow down on the more demanding passages and speed up on the easier ones, causing their listeners to feel uncomfortable. It is essential that musicians choose a song that they can play without hesitation.

MAGICIANS:

It is important that magicians do *large* tricks that can be seen well from the back of the performance site. Small tricks that are good in a living room or other intimate setting are invisible to all but the people who are sitting in the first few rows.

JUGGLERS:

Juggling equipment can usually be found in magic stores. The easiest objects to juggle are:
1.   Three small, light weight (chiffon-like) squares
2.   Hoops
3.   Balls (Lacrosse balls are best for bouncing and juggling in general).

Clubs are difficult to juggle (in addition to juggling, spinning is involved). Objects of mixed shapes and weights are also difficult.

CARTOONISTS:

Cartoonists are advised to:
1.   Use a heavy, black, felt-tipped marker (so that the drawing is visible from the back row of the audience)
2.   Draw the same, large, line drawing every time (at both rehearsals and all performances.)
3.   Practice (at home) until their drawing can be completed comfortably, within the two minute time limit.

MUSIC FOR NOVELTY ACTS:

When choosing musical accompaniment for your novelty acts, think variety!

Music for silent acts:
Musical backing can help create a mood and add strength and charm to a silent act (a performer who doesn't speak while they do their act, as opposed to talking acts that may tell jokes or talk to the audience while they juggle, draw, do magic tricks…)

Cartoonists:
Music that is appropriate to the subject matter that is being sketched. Examples:
    While drawing an action hero: Stirring, triumphant sounding music.
    While drawing a tropical scene: Serene sounding music, like *"Blue Hawaii"*.

Jugglers, rope skippers, gymnasts…
Music played in a tempo that is comfortable for each particular act to work to. Perhaps a Top-40 song or a Broadway show tune such as:
    "Everything's Comin' Up Roses"
    "Oklahoma"
Or, up-tempo jazz tunes such as:
    "Avalon"
    "Limehouse Blues"

BUILDING ROUTINES:

The following applies to magicians, jugglers, martial arts demonstrators, gymnasts, acrobats…

If your performers don't have a pre-planned routine, ask them to show you their three best tricks. Then, line up their feats of skill.
    Good
    Better
    Most spectacular

COMEDIANS:

The same principle applies to comedy.
Line up comedy material:
    Joke or riddle #1:   Funny
    Joke or riddle #2:   Funnier
    Joke or riddle #3:   Funniest

Delivering punch-lines—Encourage your comedians to:
>Be loud and clear
>Be enthusiastic—Sell it!
>Don't rush—Give the audience an opportunity to laugh.

DANGEROUS ACTS:

Acts that are dangerous to the performers should be viewed carefully and possibly omitted. (Performers would be recast.)
>Pogo sticks
>Unicycles
>Roller blades
>Skateboards...

Be alert to the fact that amateurs, particularly kids, might be stimulated by the audience to over-reach their regular safety margins and out-do themselves with dangerous results.

Watch out for acts that are messy due to water spilling. When water or other substances are spilled, it creates a hazardous condition for the acts that are to follow.

ADDITIONAL MC OPTIONS:

>The mayor
>A radio or television personality
>A local sports celebrity
>Someone from your sponsoring organization...

(Sample show #2—Celebrating Clarksville's MC is a hypothetical police agent from the sponsoring organization.)

ALL-PURPOSE SHOWS:

All production sessions; the audition and the rehearsals are held in the *evening*.

ORDER OF THE ALL-PURPOSE AUDITION:

The only crew members who are needed at the audition are the three green-room supervisors who will assist the director by:
>Greeting and organizing performers
>Keeping the green-room clutter free

Making sure that performers are completely ready when it's their turn to audition.

Sample Group One—Celebrating Clarksville: Meets at 6PM

Group One consists of: *School safety patrol members* representing 10 schools in the district. (Acts with the most people in them audition first.)

Color guard	5
Rope skippers	5
Comedians	2
Comedian	1
Comedian	1
Comedian	1
Vocalist	1
Vocalist	1
Vocalist	1
Harmonica player	1
10 Acts	*19 People*

Sample Group Two—Celebrating Clarksville: Meets at 7PM

Group two consists of: *Police personnel and their families.*

Igorot tribal dancers *(Philippines)*	3	Police officer's nieces
Country vocalists	3	Police officer and twin sons
Comedian	1	Police agent's son
Comedian	1	Police agent (MC)
Jazz vocalist	1	Police officer's daughter
Tuba player	1	Police officer
Fiddler	1	Police officer
Magician	1	Police officer
Juggler	1	Police officer
9 Acts	*13 Performers*	

Sample Group Three—Celebrating Clarksville: Meets at 8PM

Sample group three consists of: *Guest Artists.*

Fashion show models	12	Dance Studio
Flamenco	10	Dance Studio
Irish cloggers	10	Dance Studio

Cheerleaders	10	High School
Can-Can dancers	6	Dance Studio
Hip-hop dancers	6	High School
Vocal/dance act	3	High School
Tap-dancer	1	Dance Studio
8 Acts	*58 Performers*	

CHAPTER EIGHT

GETTING READY TO REHEARSE

STEP 6: HOW TO LINE UP YOUR SHOW

How you line up your show can either make or break your presentation. The show business expressions, "opening act, tough act to follow, next to closing and big finish" bring to mind ideas concerning the line-up. A good line-up is not directly noticed by the audience, but is necessary in order to:

> Get the audience's attention
> Keep it
> Build to a strong conclusion

1. Arrange the sign-up sheets into five stacks according to the five categories of acts:

Stack #1:	Movement/Dance
Stack #2:	Comedy
Stack #3:	Vocal
Stack #4:	Instrumental
Stack #5:	Novelty

2. Within each of these five stacks, organize the sign-up sheets according to *the placement code*. (The placement code can be found in the section that is titled: *"The Director's Notations"* on the sign-up sheet.

    The sign-up sheet with the lowest placement code total, *in each category*, is placed at the bottom of each stack.

    The sign-up sheet with the next to lowest placement code total, *in each category*, is placed on top of the first one, and so forth.

ORDER OF APPEARANCE—SAMPLE CHART #1:

The hypothetical *Rogers Revue* has a total of twenty-five acts. Therefore, there are twenty-five lines on this chart.

1. <u>Opening act</u> _____
2. _____
3. _____
4. _____
5. _____
6. _____
7. _____
8. _____
9. _____
10. _____
11. _____
12. _____
13. _____
14. _____
15. _____
16. _____
17. _____
18. _____
19. _____
20. _____
21. _____
22. _____
23. _____
24. <u>*Next-to-closing*</u> _____
25. <u>Closing act</u> _____

Please keep in mind, placement totals are relative. A high total simply means that one dance act (for instance) may be more proficient than all the other dance acts in that particular show

Placement Code:

The lowest possible placement code total is:	3
The highest possible placement code total is:	15

NEXT TO CLOSING:

When lining up a show, the *"next to closing"* (the next to the last) act is selected first. This place on the program is considered to be *"the star spot"*.

The performer with the highest placement total (of any act, in any category) is given the next to closing place on the program.

Next-to-closing—The Rogers Revue:
The nine-year-old Elvis impersonator, *(novelty act)* meets the qualification of having the highest rating of any act in any category. Therefore, he is placed next to closing.
On line #24, the director writes: *Elvis Impersonator, Arnie Prince.*

YOUR CLOSING ACT:

The last act on the program is selected next.

Your closing act should be the showiest, most colorful act from your movement/dance category. Ideally, it should have at least five very energetic people in it.

Closing act—The Rogers Revue:
The seven teachers, who are doing a 50's dance, meet the preceding qualifications. They will be the closing act.
On line #25, the director writes: *The Surfin' Sensations*

YOUR OPENING ACT:

Your opening (first) act is selected next. This act should be from the dance/ movement category; *gymnastics, acrobatics or aerobics preferred* (rather than dance). This act should consist of *at least three people and have a high rating.*

Act #1 should be a very energetic attention-getting act. Their music should be fast and exciting.

Opening act—The Rogers Revue:
The gymnasts meet the requirements of being a very energetic, attention getting act. They will work to fast *(samba)* music.
On line #1 the director writes: *The Gomez Gymnasts*

YOUR SECOND ACT:

This is a very important time slot. Act #2 is the act that helps convince the audience that the show will be very exciting and entertaining.

Act #2 should be a single dancer with a very high placement total who works to fast, stirring music. However, their music and presentation should contrast strongly, in style, to the opening act.

Act #2—The Rogers Revue:
Tahitian dancer, nine-year-old Leilani Owens has a very vivacious personality and works to lively, rhythmic, drum accompaniment.
    On line #2 the director writes: *Tahitian dancer, Leilani Owens*

YOUR THIRD ACT:

Your third act should be a comedy act.

Act #3 Select the act that has the second to highest (comedy) placement total.

Act #3—The Rogers Revue:
    On line #3 the director writes:
    Stand-up comedian, Yolanda Gillette

So far, the first act has the ability to get the audience's attention. The second act has the potential to delight and exhilarate them. The third act gives them an opportunity to smile (or at best, have a good belly-laugh.)

YOUR FOURTH ACT:

Act # 4 is chosen from the vocal category and has the second to highest (vocal) placement total.

Act #4—The Rogers Revue:
    On line #4 the director writes:
    Country vocalists, The Nelson Sisters

By the time the fourth act has finished performing, it has been proven to the audience that they are going to thoroughly enjoy themselves.

BUILDING IN THE AREAS OF PROFICIENCY AND SHOWMANSHIP:

The placement code totals drop to the lowest total for the fifth act. At this point, the audience is relaxed and happy and ready to appreciate the bravery of the less proficient performers. From there, the totals gradually increase. This causes the show to subtly build in strength and showmanship as it rolls along towards its victorious conclusion.

ORDER OF APPEARANCE—THE ROGERS REVUE—SAMPLE CHART #2:

Placement code totals:

1. *The Gomez Gymnasts* (Highest movement total) 12
2. *Tahitian dancer—Leilani Owens* (Highest dance total) 14
3. *Comedian—Yolanda Gillette* (2nd to highest comedy total) 13
4. *Country singers—The Nelson Sisters* (2nd to highest vocal total) 13
5.
6.
7.
8.
9.
10.
11.
12.
13.
14.
15.
16.
17.
18.
19.
20.
21.
22.
23.
24. *Elvis Impersonator—Arnie Prince* (Most charismatic of all) 15
25. *50's Dancers—The Surfin' Sensations* (Most colorful dance) 13

Expect to make at least two tries at lining up your show. After seeing the total picture, it will gradually become obvious what adjustments need to be made in order to insure that your show maintains its energy and builds as it moves along

WHERE TO PLACE YOUR MOVEMENT/DANCE ACTS:

Your movement/dance acts should be placed in the #1 spot, the #2 spot, the closing spot and at intervals throughout your show; *whenever a jolt of energy is needed.*

MOVEMENT/DANCE ACTS—THE ROGERS REVUE—SAMPLE CHART #3:

Placement code totals:

1. *Gymnasts*   12
2. *Tahitian dancer*   14
3. _____
4. _____
5. *Break dancers*   6
6. _____
7. _____
8. _____
9. _____
10. _____
11. _____
12. *Russian folk dancers*   9
13. _____
14. _____
15. _____
16. *Chinese ribbon dancers*   10
17. _____
18. *Ballet dancer*   11
19. _____
20. *Swing dancers*   12
21. _____
22. _____
23. *Hip-hop dancers*   13
24. _____
25. *50's dancers*   13

WHERE TO PLACE COMEDY ACTS:

Sprinkle humor throughout your show. Don't allow too much time to elapse before presenting something that is funny.

COMEDY ACTS—THE ROGERS REVUE—SAMPLE CHART #4:

Placement code totals:

1. _____
2. _____
3. *Comedian—Yolanda Gillette* _____ 13
4. _____
5. _____
6. *Comedian—John Paris* _____ 6
7. _____
8. _____
9. *Comedian—Jose Salazar* _____ 8
10. _____
11. _____
12. _____
13. *Comedian—Freddie Wong* _____ 10
14. _____
15. _____
16. _____
17. *(Funny act—novelty category—Ventriloquist)* _____
18. _____
19. _____
20. _____
21. *Comedians—Mandy & Joey Epstein* _____ 14
22. _____
23. _____
24. _____
25. _____

COMEDY
The premiss or essence of a comedy sketch should be established
in the first line and delivered *clearly* so that the audience gets the point
and understands what the comedian is driving at.

WHERE TO PLACE VOCALISTS:

Vocalists are usually placed after comedy acts. The reason: The audiences' ears need time to adjust to the (often) quieter sounds of vocalists. Comedians not only provide laughter, they also act as a buffer between loud acts and quieter ones.

VOCALISTS—THE ROGERS REVUE—SAMPLE CHART #5

Placement code totals:

1. _____
2. _____
3. Comedian _____
4. *Vocalists—Nelson Sisters*   13
5. _____
6. Comedian _____
7. *Vocalist—Timothy Blake*   9
8. _____
9. Comedian _____
10. *Vocalist—Ida Lumet*   10
11. _____
12. _____
13. Comedian _____
14. *Vocalist—Tyra Washington*   12
15. _____
16. _____
17. _____
18. _____
19. _____
20. _____
21. Comedians _____
22. *Vocalist—Jenny Zimmer*   14
23. _____
24. _____
25. _____

PLACING INSTRUMENTALISTS (See Chart #7):

In our sample show, *The Rogers Revue,* there are two instrumentalists. Notice how each instrumentalist's style of music contrasts to the preceding act's music.

A flutist who plays *classical* music, is placed after a *R&B* singer

A trumpet player who plays a *jazz* tune is placed after a *ballerina.*

PLACING NOVELTY ACTS: When a complete change of pace is desired, consider choosing a novelty act to fill the spot.

NOVELTY ACTS—SAMPLE CHART #6:   *Placement code totals:*

1. _____
2. _____
3. _____
4. _____
5. _____
6. _____
7. _____
8. *Baton twirler—Diedra Obaji*   7
9. _____
10. _____
11. *Mime—Florence Jordan*   8
12. _____
13. _____
14. _____
15. _____
16. _____
17. *Ventriloquist—Jimmy Cruz*   10
18. _____
19. _____
20. _____
21. _____
22. _____
23. _____
24. *Elvis Impersonator—Arnie Prince*   15
25. _____

ORDER OF APPEARANCE—THE ROGERS REVUE—SAMPLE CHART #7:

Placement code totals:

1. The Gomez Gymnasts — *12*
2. Tahitian Dancer—Leilani Owens — *14*
3. Stand-up Comedian—Yolanda Gillette — *13*
4. Country Singers—The Nelson Sisters — *13*
5. Break Dancers—The Rodriquez Brothers — *6*
6. Stand-up Comedian—John Paris — *6*
7. Irish Balladeer—Timothy Blake — *7*
8. Baton Twirler—Diedra Obaji — *7*
9. Stand-up Comedian—Jose Salazar — *8*
10. French Chanteuse—Ida Lumet — *8*
11. Mime—Florence Jordan — *8*
12. Russian Folk Dancers—Rudenko — *9*
13. Stand-up Comedian—Freddie Wong — *10*
14. Rhythm & Blues Singer—Tyra Washington — *10*
15. Flutist—Akira Kimura — *10*
16. Carmen McCormick's Chinese Ribbon Dancers — *10*
17. Ventriloquist—Jimmy Cruz — *10*
18. Ballerina—Emily Woo — *11*
19. Trumpeter—Eileen O'Connor — *11*
20. Mimi Dorsey's Swing Dancers — *12*
21. Comedians—Mandy & Joey Epstein — *14*
22. Vocalist—Jenny Zimmer — *14*
23. Rapper—Tyrone Brown and the West Side Hip-Hop Crew — *13*
24. Elvis Impersonator—Arnie Prince — *15*
25. 50's Dancers—The Surfin' Sensations — *14*

STEP 7: HOW TO WRITE YOUR CUE SHEET

The cue sheet is written by the director and read by the MC
A well-written cue sheet contains short, dynamic introductions to each act
The cue sheet gives the show continuity.

Three Typical Introductions:
And now, here's a student of Olivia Ortega at the Rising Star Studio.
She has danced at numerous recitals and family events.
Last summer she performed at the Del Mar Fair.
Please welcome—**LEILANI OWENS!**

Next, get ready to laugh, 'cause here comes—**PEDRO SANTANA!**

Hip-hop has become very popular in recent years.
It's a type of dancing that is mostly self-taught.
Our next act is headed by Rapper, Tyrone Brown.
Here's—
TYRONE BROWN AND THE WEST SIDE HIP-HOP CREW!

THE FOUR ELEMENTS OF A GOOD INTRODUCTION:
Attention-getter
Relevant data
Cue preparation
Cue

1.   *The Attention-Getter:*
The attention-getter is simply that. It is a polite sound like saying "Ah-hem." Its purpose is to re-direct the audience's attention back to the MC after the applause of the previous act.

Keep in mind that the MC is speaking to a room full of over a hundred people who may still be applauding, laughing or talking to each other about what they have just seen. The MC needs to get the attention back in order to properly introduce the next act and keep the show moving.

The most common attention-getter is the phrase *"And now"* as used in the first typical introduction.
In the second introduction, the attention-getting word is *"Next."*
In the third introduction the attention-getter is a whole sentence, *"Hip-Hop has become very popular in recent years."* This sentence is really a throw-away-line (see glossary.)

Some other attention-getters:
"Let's get the show started with…"
"At this time…"
"The next act…"
"Our next performer…"
"Here is…"
"Here's a student of…"

"Let's keep right on going with…"
"Thank you (previous performer's name)…"
"The performer(s) in our next act…"

2.   *Relevant Data:*
     This information can be found on the sign-up sheets.
     In the first example of a typical introduction, Leilani had written about her private lessons and her performing experience. This made it possible for the director to write a good introduction.
>   It gave credit to Olivia Ortega, *her dance teacher*
>   It mentioned the *Rising Star Studio.* This is good public relations.
>   By mentioning private teachers, studios and programs for children, the show becomes, in part, a source of information about local activities.
>   Pointing out that Leilani has danced at numerous family get-togethers and recitals is a nice build-up.
>   Her appearance at the Del Mar Fair, a well-known event, acknowledges her community involvement.

In the second introduction, the most relevant information about Pedro is the fact that he is going to tell jokes.
>   Here, the second element is *"get ready to laugh."* It tells the audience that they are about to see a comedian.

In the third introduction for the West Side Hip-Hop Crew, the second element is, *"it is a type of dance that is mostly self-taught. Our next act is headed by Tyrone Brown."*
>   The second sentence in the third example of a typical introduction implies that the boys thought up the act themselves.
>   The third sentence points out that Tyrone is in charge of the group. Obviously, he is a motivator and deserves to be acknowledged for his leadership abilities.

It often happens with acts consisting of several people, that the sign-up sheets each include different bits of relevant data about each person.
Suppose that one wrote that they were in a school play, another indicated they had previously danced with a different group, and yet another member of the act, mentioned that they had performed at a festival.
Desirable as it might be to mention all these accomplishments, it makes for a very unwieldy introduction. It is better to focus on the group leader of the particular act, in the above case, Tyrone Brown.

3.   *The Cue Preparation:*

The cue preparation is a readiness alert. It is equivalent to "On your marks, get set..."

> For Leilani it's *"Please welcome..."*
> For Pedro it's *"cause here comes..."*
> For Tyrone Brown and the West Side Hip-Hop Crew it's H*ere's..."*

Additional Cue Preparations:

> "Open the curtain for..."
> "Let's..."
> "It's..."
> "They call their act..."
> "Please watch..."
> "Please listen to..."
> "Get ready for..."
> "Put your hands together for..."
> "Let's bring on..."
> "Give it up for..."

4.   *The Cue:*

The cue is the action word or phrase to which the crew and performers respond:

The first example:	"<u>LEILANI OWENS</u>!"
The second example:	"<u>PEDRO SANTANA</u>!"
The third example:	"<u>TYRONE BROWN AND THE WEST SIDE HIP-HOP CREW</u>!"

STAGE MARKINGS—SIGHT-LINES AND PERFORMANCE BOUNDARIES:

The stage markings provide reference points that make it possible for your performers to quickly get their bearings.

Center stage:

The director marks the center of the stage by placing a length of painter's masking tape *(front to back—in a direct line)* from the center-front edge of the stage or performing area, to the center-back of the backdrop.

This marking helps performers position themselves so that they can present a more aesthetically pleasing picture to the audience.

Back boundary:
The back boundary is marked by placing a length of painter's masking tape *across* the stage. It is placed three-quarters of the distance between the front edge of the stage or performing area and the backdrop. *(See Auditorium set-up chart—next page).*

The reason for the back boundary:
Instead of allowing your performers to draw back or try to hide out on the back portion of the stage (which is often the tendency).

> This boundary places performers where the lighting is most effective and flattering.
>
> Performers are automatically brought forward, making it easier for them to connect with the audience.

Acts that require more space (for instance—the thirty swing dancers in *The Rogers Revue)* are allowed to use the area beyond the back boundary.

SAMPLE SET-UP CHART – A TYPICAL AUDITORIUM

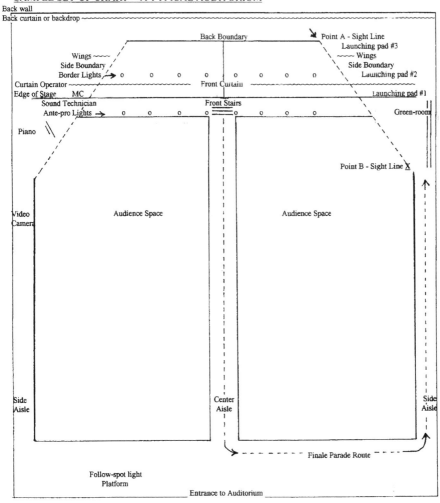

How to determine the back boundary end points:
1.   Place a chair 12 feet back from the front edge of the stage and 3 feet away from the side wall of the auditorium. *(See Point B Sight-line—Auditorium set-up chart).*
2.   Ask a volunteer to stand on the stage on the back boundary and move toward the side wall *(stage left).*
3.   At the instant the volunteer moves out of sight say, *"stop!"*
4.   Ask your volunteer to reverse direction and take one step towards center-stage (so they are once again in full view). This place will be the end point of the back boundary *(stage-left).*
5.   Using a yardstick, measure the distance from *center-stage* to the *stage-left* end point. Then measure the equal distance from *center-stage* to where the *stage-right* end point should be. Tear the tape at this point so that both end-points match.
6.   Remove the portion of the *center-stage* tape that goes from the *back boundary to the backdrop.* This preliminary marking is no longer needed.

Sight-lines and the resulting (side) boundaries:
1.   Ask your volunteer to stand at the *end point* of the *stage-left* back boundary and hold one end of a piece of string at floor (stage) level.
2.   Hold the other end of the string and walk back to the *Point B-sight-line* position.
3.   While you and your volunteer hold the string taut and level, ask your volunteer to *anchor it* with tape at the *back boundary end point* and again at the *edge of the stage.*
4.   Mark the *sight-line/side boundary (next to the string)* with a length of tape that extends from the *stage-left* end point to the *front edge of the stage.*
5.   Duplicate this sight-line/side boundary marking on the opposite side of the stage.

The side boundaries remind performers to stay within the sight lines so that during their act everyone in the audience will be able to see them.

Audience space—Sight-lines:
1.   Anchor the sight-line string *directly below the edge of the stage on the auditorium floor* (at the place that is in line with the point A and point B sight-line positions).
2.   Anchor the string again at the Point B sight-line location *(indicated by the X on the Auditorium set-up chart).*
3.   Place a length of tape along the sight-line on the auditorium floor.
4.   Repeat this step on the opposite side of the auditorium.
5.   Remove the string.

The sight-line markings on the auditorium floor make it clear to the custodian exactly where to set up the chairs for the audience.

After the sight-lines have been charted, you can rest assured that every seat sold will be a *"good"* seat, with an unobstructed view.

The curtain line:
Mark the curtain line with a length of tape.
The curtain line reminds performers (who use the full stage) of the curtain's path. It alerts them, so they can avoid the awkwardness and embarrassment of having the curtain collide with them when it closes.

The Auditorium Set-up Chart also indicates:
> Launching pad locations
> Curtain operator's (usual) location
> MC's microphone location
> Sound technician's location
> Center aisle
> Center-front stairs for the finale parade
> Piano/electronic keyboard location
> Green-room location
> Side aisle—video camera location
> Side aisle—finale parade return route
> Follow-spotlight platform location

FORMULATING YOUR TECHNICAL WORKSHEET

The entire crew works from copies of the same technical worksheet.
The horizontal lines on the technical worksheet that divide the show into segments are observed at the first rehearsal only.
> School shows are divided into three parts for the first rehearsal
> All-purpose shows are divided into two parts for the first rehearsal.

Act#		Props	Tapes	Microphone set-ups
(1)	Gymnasts-Gomez	*3 Gym mats*	T	
(2)	Dancer-Owens		T-L/M	
3	Comedian-Gillette			HHM
4	Vocalists-Nelson	*2 Guitars*		2M/S
(5)	Dancers-Rodriguez		T	
6	Comedian-Paris			HHM
7	Vocalist-Blake		T-L/M	HHM
(8)	Baton-Obaji	*Baton*	T	
9	Comedian-Salazar			HHM
10	Vocalist-Lumet		T-L/M	HHM
11	Mime-Jordan			
12	Comedian-Wong			HHM
13	Vocalist-Washington		T-L/M	HHM
(14)	Dancers-Rudenko		T-L/M	
15	Flutist-Akira	*Flute-music stand*		M/S
(16)	Dancers-McCormick	*3 streamers*	T	
17	Ventriloquist-Cruz	*Dummy & stool*		M/S
(18)	Dancer-Wong		T	
19	Trumpet-O'Connor	*Trumpet*	T-L/M	M/S
(BD-20)	Dancers-Dorsey		T	
21	Comedians-Epstein			M/S
22	Vocalist-Zimmer		T-L/M	HHM
(D-23)	Rap/Hip-Hop-Brown		T	HHM
24	Impersonator-Prince		T	HHM
(BD-25)	Dancers-Sensations	*3 Surfboards*	T	

SAMPLE TECHNICAL WORKSHEET: **THE ROGERS REVUE**

The technical worksheet will be explained in detail in the next chapter—Meeting With Your Crew

Most professional performers and musicians
are more than willing to contribute their time
and talent to a cause they believe in.

SAMPLE TECHNICAL WORKSHEET

CELEBRATING CLARKSVILLE

There is no front curtain at this hypothetical show site. For this reason, brackets around act numbers that signify an open curtain, are omitted.

All musical accompaniment will be live

This sample show has a musical director/keyboard player, who will be present at the audition, both rehearsals and all performances to accompany any act that uses music, therefore cassette tapes will not be needed for this show.

LM = Live music

Act #		Props	Live Music	Microphone set-ups
Pre-show	Color Guard	Flag		M/S
Pre-show	National Anthem		LM	HHM
1	Rope-Skippers-Romanoff	Ropes	LM	M/P
2	Tap-dancer-Jenkins		LM	M/P
3	Comedian-Anderson			HHM
4	Vocal/dance-Watson		LM	HHM
5	Harmonica player-Rich		LM	M/S
6	Tribal Dancers-Gutierrez		LM	
7	Comedian-Christianson			HHM
8	Vocalist-Hutton		LM	HHM
9	Cheerleaders-Kilbran	Pom Poms	LM	M/S
10	Tuba player-Michaelson	Tuba	LM	M/S
11	Comedian-Zarnow Jr.			HHM
12	Vocalist-Kaye		LM	HHM
13	Clog dancers-Parton		LM	M/P
14	Magician-Blake	Prop table		M/S
15	Vocalist-DeVincenzo		LM	HHM
16	Comedian-Henson			HHM
17	Fashion show-Horne		LM	M/S
18	Country fiddler-Andrews	Violin	LM	M/S
19	Hip-Hop dancers-Nichols		LM	
20	Comedians-Ming & Long			M/S
21	Juggler-Harmon	Balls, clubs	LM	
22	Comedian-Zarnow			HHM
23	Flamenco troupe-Garcia	3 chairs		
	(Consisting of:	3 guitars		
	6 dancers			M/P
	3 guitarists			
	1 vocalist)			M/S
24	Cancan dancers-Marceau		LM	M/S

The time and effort it takes to formulate your technical worksheet can save you, your crew and performers, hours of wasted time later on. Everyone involved won't have to be kept waiting while the director decides how to stage the various acts.

Many staging details can be thought-out during the eight days between the audition and the first rehearsal. Most of the information you need has already been gathered. (Refer to *Director's Notations*—Sign-up Sheets).

If an act uses a cassette tape, that is listed

The space an act needs is listed:
> Either they work on the front portion of the stage or they use the full stage.

If an act uses a prop, that is listed.

If an act requires a microphone set up, the type of set-up is listed.

SETTING UP DECISIONS

The following equipment should *always* be set up on the opposite side of the performance site from the green-room:
Mc's microphone
Sound technician's table
Piano or electronic keyboard and bench
Video camera and tripod
Follow-spotlight and platform

The objective is to keep the MC, curtain operator, sound technician, sound technician's assistant, accompanists, video camera operator and follow-spotlight operators well away from the launching pads and the finale parade route.

Where do you place the equipment listed above?

If you have a front curtain and plan to use it, the location of the curtain control is the determining factor. (The MC's microphone, piano, etc., should be set up on the same side of the performance site as the curtain control.)

Curtain control type #1:	The opening and closing of most front curtains is controlled by pulling downward on a rope that passes over a grooved wheel or rope pulley.
Curtain control type #2:	Some front curtains are controlled by pressing a button.

If you don't have a front curtain at your performance site, either side of the performance site could be used for the MC's microphone, etc. However, if at all possible *use the side that has no, or fewer, doors.*

We suggest that you post signs on all side doors that say "Emergency exit only"

The only door that should be used during rehearsals and performances is the one that is at, or near, the rear of the performance site.

CHAPTER NINE

MEETING WITH YOUR CREW

The ideal time to meet with your crew is the day before your first rehearsal.

Objective: Familiarize your crew with the technical worksheet.

At the beginning of this meeting and before each rehearsal and performance, your crew members are supplied with:

Their own personal copy of the technical worksheet. (They are asked to write their name at the top right-hand corner.)

A pencil with an eraser

Your three green-room supervisors are each supplied with a technical worksheet and a clipboard.

At the end of this meeting, after each rehearsal and each performance, the director collects the technical worksheets and the clipboards.

YOUR GREEN-ROOM SUPERVISORS:

Your green-room supervisors are asked to discuss among themselves and decide who would like to be in charge of the following:

1. One supervisor will be in charge of entrances. (This supervisor helps performers get to their specific entry point on time.)
2. The second green-room supervisor will be in charge of exits. (When an act has finished performing, this supervisor guides them back to the green-room.)
3. The third supervisor will be in charge of reminding performers to move. (Sometimes performers are so enthralled with watching the show, they forget to go where they're supposed to go and need a *gentle* reminder.)

Your green-room supervisor's focus:
The green-room supervisors are cross trained so that if need be; they can fill in for each other. The brackets, omission of brackets, and the letter "B" that precedes some act numbers, let your greenroom supervisors know where to send the various performers for their entrances.

1. If there are *no* brackets around an act number, send that act to launching pad #1.
2. If there *are* brackets around an act number, send that act backstage.
3. If there is a "B" in front of an act number, that act will be entering from the *back* of the performance site.

PERFORMANCE SITE LAYOUTS:

Some auditoriums are designed in such a way that one must go outside of the building in order to go backstage. Other auditoriums have entryways within the auditorium providing easy access to the backstage area.

Layout A:
If there *is* backstage access within your performance site, you will have four entrance options:
>   Launching pad #1
>   Launching pad #2
>   Launching pad #3 (Used primarily for the finale parade)
>   From the back of the performance site.

Layout B:
If there is *no direct access to backstage,* you will have two entrance options:
>   Launching pad #1
>   From the back of the performance site.

We suggest that you limit the back of the performance site entrance to three acts at most. This type of entrance can create a delightful change; however, because of the time it takes to travel all the way up the center aisle, it can become tedious if done more than three times.

YOUR CURTAIN OPERATOR:

1. Demonstrate how to open and close the front curtain using a steady, fairly fast, hand-over-hand technique.
   The objective is to pull down on the rope with a continuous motion and open and close the curtain smoothly.
   A choppy motion, in addition to being unsightly, could derail the curtain.
2. The curtain should be opened and closed fairly quickly, but not so fast as to cause it to swish and knock things over; namely props or a microphone stand. So you can see whether or not your instructions have been understood, ask your curtain operator to open and close the curtain.

3.   The curtain is opened for those acts whose number is bracketed *only*. *No bracket—No curtain.*

4.   The only time a slow curtain is used in *Talent Shows the Kent Way* is when something poignant has just been presented and a fast curtain would break the mood.

5.   Explain that the curtain is opened *after* the cue has been said. It's important not to *"jump the gun"* and open the curtain too soon. The reasons: It would take the audience's attention away from the MC. The sound that the curtain makes as it opens, would partially drown out what the MC is saying.

6.   Suggest gloves to prevent blisters. Suede gardening gloves, purchased at a hardware store, work well.

7.   Explain that when it's time for the curtain to close, *it should be closed even if some of the performers are in its path.* The curtain will touch them this time, but next time they will be more aware.

8.   The same holds true for opening the curtain on cue, but before the act on stage is ready. Next time they *will* be ready.

The curtain operator is also in charge of the backstage house lights dimmer-switch. (The cue for operating this switch will be discussed later.)

Curtain cue code—Your curtain operator's focus:

1.   *Brackets:*
     Brackets are placed around an act's number if that particular act requires an open curtain.

2.   *A Delayed Curtain:*
     When the director decides to combine two acts, this treatment works well. A *"D"* in front of an act's number stands for a *Delayed* curtain and alerts the curtain operator to wait for a second cue, before opening the curtain.
     An example:
     The opening of the curtain for Act #23 (D-23) *The Rogers Revue* will be delayed. Tyrone starts the act by rapping (alone) in front of the closed curtain, for about thirty seconds. At the completion of Tyrone's solo rap, the curtain opens to reveal his hip-hop dancers.
     (At the first rehearsal, the director will ask the curtain operator to write the curtain cue on her technical worksheet. In the above case, the cue to open the curtain is the last phrase that Tyrone says at the end of his solo rap).

3.   *The letters "BD" in front of an act's number mean:*
     This act will be entering from the *Back* of the performance site and the curtain will be *Delayed.*

An example:
Act (BD-20) *Mimi Dorsey's Swing Dancers* and Act (BD-25) *The Surfin'
Sensations,* will enter from the <u>*Back*</u> of the auditorium and will require a <u>*Delayed*</u>
curtain. (The curtain cue, in the above cases, will be a *visual* cue. When the first
person from each of these acts reaches the bottom step, of the center-front
stairs, the curtain operator is instructed to open the front curtain.)

YOUR STAGE MANAGER:

Before each rehearsal and performance begins, the director does a *"prop check"*
with the stage manager to make sure that all props listed on the technical worksheet are accounted for.

The stage manager:

Sets props	Places, or helps to place, performing equipment on the stage
Strikes props	Removes, or helps to remove, performing equipment from the stage.

Your stage manager's focus:
1. All props are listed on the technical worksheet. This alerts the stage manager
    so that he or she will know which acts will require prop set-ups.
2. The brackets around an act's number alert the stage manager to the fact that
    these particular acts will be coming backstage for their entrances.
    Most acts (who are sent backstage) will wait on launching pad #2 until
    they are introduced, or until it's time for them to go to their center-
    stage starting place. (The director makes this clear at the first
    rehearsal.)
    Launching pad #3. In addition to being used for the finale parade, this
    point of entry can also be used for a fashion show or the costume
    parade. At the first rehearsal, the stage manager will be asked by the
    director to mark his or her technical worksheet accordingly. (In sample
    show, *The Rogers Revue,* the only time that launching pad #3 is used is
    for the finale parade. In sample show, *Celebrating Clarksville,* launching
    pad #3 is used for a fashion show and the finale parade.)

YOUR SOUND TECHNICIAN:

*It is important that a separate cassette tape is used for each act that uses recorded
music or sound effects. In the event that an act is absent, this method makes it possible to make adjustments quickly and easily by simply removing one act's tape.*

The space should be maintained however, so that when the act returns for the next performance, their tape can be positioned once again in its proper place

(Extra-short, inexpensive cassette tapes can be purchased from: Tape Repair & Sales, San Diego, CA (619) 299-0088) E-mail: taperepair@earthlink.net

Your sound technician's focus:
1.   Taped musical accompaniment is indicated by placing the letter *"T"* in the *"tape column"* on the technical worksheet. This alerts the sound technician so that he or she will know which acts require cassette tapes.
      T-L/M: This abbreviation indicates that a cassette *Tape* will be used at rehearsals and *Live Music* will be provided at performances.
2.   The sound technician also pays attention to the microphone set-up column. While microphones are being moved from one place to another, the volume is turned off so that the sounds made while the microphone is in transit are not heard. As soon as the microphone set-up is completed, the sound technician re-adjusts the sound levels.
3.   Acts that enter from the back of the performance site require a longer musical introduction. Instead of the usual four bar introduction that most acts receive, these acts will probably need a sixteen bar introduction.
4.   When the microphone is laid on the front edge of the stage for the purpose of amplifying floor sounds, increase the treble so that the sounds will be crisp.

YOUR SOUND ASSISTANT:
1.   Between microphone set-ups, the sound assistant sits at the sound technician's table. The performer's microphone is situated on a stand close by. *The sound assistant is asked to return the performer's microphone to this location after each use.*
2.   Demonstrate how to adjust the microphone stand to various heights by loosening and tightening the ring on the stand that was designed for this purpose. Tighten it just enough so that the microphone stand maintains its height, without slipping.
3.   The sound assistant should not be shy about going to the stage after an act has started in order to re-adjust the height of the microphone if it is wrong. It is better to have a slight interruption than awkwardness for a whole act.
4.   Demonstrate how to remove the microphone from its stand when a hand-held microphone is needed.
      When providing a hand-held microphone, the sound assistant should meet the performer as he or she arrives (usually) front and center.

If there is a stage at your performance site, the assistant is instructed to stand on the auditorium floor next to the center stairs, and hand *up* the microphone to the performer when he or she arrives center-stage.

The microphone could be placed on the floor ready to be picked up by the performer, but we feel it is more dignified to have the sound assistant give the microphone to the performer personally.

5. Demonstrate the tilting feature of the microphone adaptor clip and explain that the microphone should not be angled down or *it might slip out.*
6. Show the sound assistant how to place the microphone on a cushion on the center-front edge of the stage for the amplification of floor sounds.
7. When carrying the microphone on the microphone stand, the assistant is asked to use both hands:
   One hand holding the microphone stand and the other hand holding the microphone itself.
8. Be aware that the microphone's cord must be kept *untangled.*

Your sound assistant's focus:
When a microphone is needed, the following abbreviations tell what type of set-up is required:
1. HHM: *Hand-Held Microphone*
   When acts, (vocalists and stand-up comedians, for instance) have the mobility that a hand-held microphone offers them; they are able to move around freely on the stage.
2. M/S: *Microphone on a Stand*
   The following performers in our sample show, *The Rogers Revue,* do not have a free hand to hold a microphone.
   Therefore, they will need a microphone stand.
      Act#4: A vocal/guitar act (They use both hands for playing their guitars.)
      Act #15: Flutist (He uses both hands for playing his flute.)
      Act #19: Trumpeter (She uses both hands for playing her trumpet.)
      Act #17: Ventriloquist (He uses one hand to manipulate his dummy and the other for gesturing.
3. M/P: *Microphone on a Pillow*
   When the amplification of floor sounds is desired, the microphone is placed on a cushion (front and center) near the edge of the stage.

YOUR FOLLOW-SPOTLIGHT OPERATORS:

General instructions:

1.   Do not light up anything that is irrelevant (such as a guitar player's feet).
2.   When an act is introduced, pan (move horizontally) from the MC to the entering act.
3.   Follow the action smoothly (without jiggling).
4.   When an act exists, after following them off-stage, pan back to the MC. (After performing, all acts exit the same side as the green-room, usually stage-left).
5.   Alternate spotlight operators every four or five acts so that each operator has a chance to sit down rest and cool off. (This task is hot, tiring and requires standing.)
6.   The spotlight operators are asked to decide between themselves when to spell each other off. However, *once decided they should be consistent so that each is on duty for the same acts every time.*
7.   Demonstrate the *iris control* that varies the size of the circle of light.

The two main circle-of-light sizes that are used for *Talent Shows the Kent Way:*
The small circle of light:
This size covers a performer from their waist to just above their head. It is used for any performer whose face and/or hands are their main focal point. Such as:

> The MC
> Vocalists
> Stand-up comics
> Musicians
> Magicians…

The medium sized circle of light:
This size covers a performer from just below their feet, to just above their head. It is used for performers who move around a lot. Such as:

> Dancers
> Gymnasts
> Very animated (physical) comics
> Martial arts demonstrators
> Baton twirlers…

What do the follow-spotlight operators do when there are *many* people in an act? The follow-spotlight operators are instructed to highlight the featured performer(s) in the group. For example:

A performer who is on stage with a large group, but is meant to be the *center of attention* at a particular time.

A singer in a chorus who takes the lead for a few bars

A challenge dancer (break, hip-hop, tap...) who does one of his or her best moves or steps, and then dares someone else in the group to do better. It's all rehearsed, of course.

Your follow-spotlight operator's focus:

The markings on the technical worksheet let the follow-spotlight operators know where to pan (move horizontally) for entrances.

1.   From the MC to launching pad #1: If an act's number is not bracketed.
2.   From the MC to center stage: For acts that begin their acts center stage. At the first rehearsal, the director will ask the spotlight operators, to mark their technical worksheets with the word, *Center,* in these cases.
3.   From the MC to the center aisle: For acts who enter from the back of the performance site. In addition to being marked on the technical worksheet with the letters "BD" (Back Delayed) this type of entrance is obvious to the spotlight operators. They can see the next act waiting nearby, for their cue to enter.

YOUR MC:

In addition to a technical worksheet, the MC is given a cue sheet.

Instructions for your MC—The power stance:

Stand with your feet about 12 inches apart.

Your weight should be evenly distributed on both feet.

Stand tall.

Hold the cue sheet in the hand that is closer to center-stage.

The MC should stand with his or her body turned toward the center of the audience.

The reason: If the MC were to stand facing directly forward (the microphone is placed at the side of the stage) it would create the feeling that only that side of the audience was being addressed. *Including the entire audience is the objective.*

1.   The MC's cue sheet should be backed with a sheet of black construction paper to avoid glare.
2.   The height of the microphone stand should be such that the microphone is just below the MC's chin. This prevents the microphone from casting a shadow on the MC's face.
3.   The microphone should be angled so that it points toward the MC's mouth.

4. *Emphasize that the crew and the act waiting to enter are depending on the clarity of the cues.*

5. When reading an introduction, the MC should not try to look at the audience like an anchor person on television. It is too difficult and unnecessary. The MC can still make a good connection with the audience by looking at them before and after reading a cue.

6. If the MC needs help with the correct pronunciation of names, they are instructed to *ask the performer in question directly,* and write the name(s) out phonetically on the cue sheet. (The MC will have a few minutes to do this at the beginning of the first rehearsal, while attendance is being taken.)

7. After introducing an act, and *before going backstage,* the MC should wait for approximately five seconds, *until the audience's attention has shifted to the act.* This shows friendliness toward the entering act and is much more polite than leaving abruptly.

8. At the end of an act, when the act *begins* to exit, the MC should hurry back to the microphone and look at the performer(s) as they exit.

Applause has a shape; it reaches its peak and (sometimes quickly, sometimes gradually) dies out. Seconds before the applause fades completely, the MC should begin to introduce the next act.

Your MC is in charge of presenting each act to the audience:
Proudly
Graciously
In a relaxed way

Mention to your MC that there will be some acts that he or she will enjoy more than others, but all performers should be introduced with equal respect.

CHAPTER TEN

THE FIRST REHEARSAL

The sound system and the follow-spotlight (if you plan to use one) are needed at this rehearsal.

OBJECTIVES:

Rehearse each act.
> *Practice:*
> Prop set-ups
> Microphone set-ups
> Introductions
> Entrances
> Exits

STAGE LIGHTING:

> If your performance site has ante-pro lights, turn them on and adjust them so that the *front section* of the stage or performing area is evenly lit.
> If your performance site has border lights, turn them on and adjust them so that the *mid-section* of the stage or performing area is evenly lit.

If you don't have the above lighting options, four photoflood lamps on stands will be necessary.
> Focus them so that two lamps illuminate the *front section* of the performing area and two lamps illuminate the *mid-section* of the performing area.

SETTING UP:

1. Post a copy of the technical worksheet near the entrance to your performance site.
2. Ask one of your green-room supervisors to alert performers as they arrive:
   > Ask performers to look at the posted copy of the technical worksheet and find out what their act number is.
   > Notice which act precedes them.

By knowing their act number and being aware of who will be seated next to them, your performers can help expedite the seating process considerably.

3.   Place the sound technician's table near the stage. *(See Auditorium set-up chart).*
4.   Place two chairs at the sound technician's table facing the stage.
     One chair should be placed at the left end of the table for the sound technician's use.
     The second chair should be placed at the right end of the table for the sound assistant's use.
5.   Set up the MC's microphone on a microphone stand (usually stage-right).
6.   Set up the performer's microphone on a microphone stand and place it next to where the sound assistant will be seated.
     The on/off switch on both microphones should be left on at all times. (The sound technician activates microphones and monitors and adjusts sound levels as needed.)
7.   Follow-spotlight:
     Position your follow-spotlight platform and the follow-spotlight at least eight feet *off-center* at the back of your location. (Shining a bright light *directly* at your performers has a tendency to dazzle them.)
     Place a chair next to the platform for the spotlight operators' use.
8.   Green-room seating: Set up about 25 chairs along the side wall of your performance site, near the stage or performing area.

BRIEFING YOUR PERFORMERS:

Time spent on the briefing should be short; ten minutes at most.
1.   At the beginning of each of the rehearsal segments, introduce the acts in that particular section of the show, to the crew.
2.   Briefly describe to your performers what the crew will be doing to help them look and sound their best.

Green-room supervisors:	Guide them to and from the stage
Sound technician:	Adjusts sound levels and starts tapes
Sound assistant:	Sets up microphones
Stage manager:	Maintains quiet and order backstage
	Sets props
Curtain operator:	Opens and closes the front curtain
Follow-spotlight operators:	Focus attention
	Follow action
MC:	Introduces them to the audience

As you introduce your crew members to your performers, show your appreciation by applauding for each one of them. Encourage your performers to applaud too.

3. Explain that the stage markings are there to help performers get situated. By staying within the boundaries, performers will automatically be in their best light and in full sight of the entire audience.

4. A volunteer is asked to stand on the curtain line. Ask your curtain operator to close the front curtain, demonstrating that if a performer is in the curtain's path when it closes, it will brush against them and produce an unwanted, awkward effect.

5. Explain how the center line will help performers with their spacing:

   If there are two performers in an act, they should position themselves, one on either side of the center tape.

   If there are three performers in an act, one works center and the others work (equally spaced) on either side.

   If there are four performers, two of them work on one side of the center tape and two of them work on the other side, and so forth.

Of course, most performers do not remain stationary while they work. The center line is just a guideline. Each performer is asked to notice where they are in relation to the center line at the beginning and at the end of their act.

6. Tell your performers that if they forget where they are supposed to go for their entrance, the green-room supervisors each have a copy of the technical worksheet and will remind them.

7. Acts who will be working on the front portion of the performing area are instructed to go to launching pad #1 immediately after the act ahead of them has made their entrance.

8. While waiting to be introduced, performers are asked to stay behind the line and be unobtrusive until it's their turn to enter.

9. When it's time for the act that is currently on stage to exit, the next act is asked to give them space, so they can get past them.

10. Acts who use the full stage and make their entrance from the middle portion of the performing area or from behind the front curtain, are instructed to:

    Go to launching pad #2 as soon as the act ahead of them has been introduced.

    They are asked to be considerate of the act who is currently on stage by being quiet.

    Stay behind the starting-line, remaining *completely* out of the audience's sight until it's their turn to go to their on-stage places.

11. Encourage performers to applaud for each other. This not only creates a cheerful atmosphere but to a degree, simulates an audience, which in turn helps the MC with his or her timing.

It is advisable to limit the total time spent on each act to a maximum of seven minutes. A kitchen timer is helpful for this. Participants have a tendency to be more focused and attentive when there is a sense of urgency.

After the performers' briefing is complete, the director asks the crew to go to their places and refer to their technical worksheets.

STEP 9: HOW TO REHEARSE EACH ACT

1. If the act uses a cassette tape, the sound technician loads the cued-up tape into the tape deck.
2. If the act has a live accompanist and the accompanist is a piano or keyboard player, he or she is asked to be seated on the piano bench, ready to begin. (If possible they should be in position one act ahead of time.)
3. The director checks to see that the act has been sent to the correct point of entry.
4. If a prop is required, the stage manager gets ready to set the prop, or gives the prop to its owner (if the performer enters carrying it.)

    If it's something that requires special handling, like a musical instrument (for example) the stage manager is instructed to let the owner takes it out of its case, him or herself.

5. The director decides the best place to set each prop and goes through the set-up process with the stage manager before the act requiring a prop is introduced. The stage manager is asked to mark his or her technical worksheet with this information so that next time there will be a clear reminder as to where to place it.

    Music stands and easels should be positioned at a 45 degree-angle, so that the musician or artist can be clearly seen.

    A magician's prop table is usually placed front and center.
6. If a microphone set-up is required, and depending on what type of set-up is indicated on the technical worksheet, the sound technician's assistant either leaves the microphone on the microphone stand or takes the microphone off the microphone stand; in anticipation of giving it to the performer.

The microphone set-up is practiced with the performer(s) once before they are officially introduced.

If a microphone stand is used, the sound technician's assistant is asked to mark her technical worksheet precisely; so that next time she will know exactly how high to raise or lower the microphone before the act makes their entrance. An easy way to do this is to use herself as a yardstick.
For example:
Eye level
Chin level
Chest level…

7. The MC is asked to get into position at the microphone, ready to introduce the act.
8. The director walks the act through their entrance:
Checks to see that acts with two or more people in them are in the correct order, so that the performer, who has to go the farthest, enters first. *Each performer is shown their exact destination* once, before they are introduced by the MC.

9. The director asks the MC to introduce the act. While the act is rehearsing, the director is completely involved and makes corrections on-the-spot while the act runs through their routine. Such as:
Louder!
Clearer!
Come closer!
Good!
Follow-spotlight:
Smaller!
Bigger!
Focus here on *this* performer!
Good!

10. After each act has rehearsed, they are not dismissed until the director:
Asks the crew if they have any questions.
Asks the performer(s) if they have any questions.

It is imperative that each child has the security of knowing:
Exactly when to go on stage
By what route
Where to be while on stage
When and how to get off stage.

Keep the rehearsal moving right along. Throughout this day your crew is learning by doing. The 1ˢᵗ rehearsal lets your cast and crew know what to expect. Soon they will hit their stride.

AN EXAMPLE OF PROP SET-UP AND STRIKE PRECISION:

Sample Show #1—The Rogers Revue:
The most difficult prop set-up, in either of our sample shows, is for act #1 in *"The Rogers Revue"*. They require three large, unwieldy, gym mats.

When the performer briefing is completed, the stage manager sets the mats for the first act:
> Gymnastic mats are usually stored on large hooks backstage.
> The three mats are placed about 10 inches behind the curtain line, end-to-end, across the stage. (Most mats have Velcro fastening strips that join them together, preventing separation.) Once the mats are in place, the director asks the curtain operator to close the front curtain.

Green-room supervisor #1 is asked to send *The Gomez Gymnasts* backstage.
> As soon as they have left to go backstage (to stretch and get ready to be introduced) the remaining performers in the green-room move up. The first act *(The Gomez Gymnasts)* occupies six chairs. As soon as those six chairs have been vacated, the next performers sit in them, and so forth.

Once an act has been introduced, they are instructed to be totally "on" (fully present) and give the audience their best.

IMPRESS YOUR WAITING PERFORMERS WITH A STRONG THEATRICAL BEGINNING:

Opening Sequence—Sample Show—The Rogers Revue:
1.   The director, using the performer's microphone, introduces the MC:

"And now it's show time!—Please welcome your Master of Ceremonies —**HEZAKIAH JONES!** *"*

2.   The cue for dimming the house lights is: *Hezakiah Jones!*
3.   At the cue, the follow-spotlight is immediately turned on and focused on Hezakiah's entrance. (He enters from behind the closed front curtain, near the curtain operator's station, *stage right.*)
4.   The director and the performers in the green-room applaud.

5. The first act is introduced.

    *"Let's get the show started with a group of athletes who were coached by
    Antonio Gomez—Open the curtain for—**THE GOMEZ GYMNASTS!**"*

6. Music—Curtain—Action!
7. During the act, the follow-spotlight is focused on whichever gymnast is
    being featured at the moment.
8. At the conclusion of their act, *The Gomez Gymnasts* do a flip and end up fac-
    ing the audience. They pose, arms extended to the ceiling, and hold that
    pose until the curtain has closed *completely*. The curtain operator writes this
    information on her worksheet.
9. Everyone in the auditorium applauds.
10. The MC re-enters.

The procedure for striking the gym mats. (Strike: Take down or remove).
    As soon as the curtain has closed, the gymnasts put away the mats; two peo-
ple to a mat.
    The stage manager assists by holding any obstructing curtains out of the way.
The gymnasts, who are closest to the mat storage hooks, put their mat away
first.
    Next, without delay, the center gymnasts place the center mat on the storage
hooks.
    Finally, the last two gymnasts put the third mat away, in immediate succession.

The removal of the mats should be repeated two or three times so that it's done
Quietly, and with precision; each time faster than the time before.

The director asks the curtain operator to open the curtain for the mat/strike
process, *(at this rehearsal only)* so that everyone in the auditorium can see what's
going on.
    The first time it might take 60 seconds
    The second time 30 seconds
    And the third time 20 seconds.
    The director congratulates the gymnasts for their speed and precision in
accomplishing this task.
    Everyone in the auditorium is encouraged to applaud and cheer.

*The opening sequence (1-10) will have to be repeated before moving on.
Establishing a confident, strong first impression is of vital importance.*

There will not be enough time for the gymnasts to cross the stage before the curtain re-opens for the next act. Therefore, they are instructed to remain where they are (out of sight) and cross over when the front curtain closes again (at the conclusion of Act #2).

PROP AND MICROPHONE SET-UPS—ALL SHOWS:

As soon as the previous act has exited, the stage manager sets the prop for the next act (if a prop is required). With the director's guidance and the performer's input, the most comfortable and effective placement is decided upon.

As soon as the stage manager has placed the prop, the sound assistant sets the microphone (if a microphone is required) and adjusts its height. All this is synchronized so that it's done in a matter of seconds.

The stage manager is asked to mark his technical worksheet *precisely*:
For example: Set 1 chair—2' back from the edge of the stage and 3' off-center (*stage left.*)

The sound technician is asked to mark her technical worksheet *precisely*:
For example:
    Microphone *front and center*—Height (her own) waist level.

The MC observes the set-up.
    Once the set-up is complete, the MC introduces the act and the act is done in its entirety.

This process is repeated until all the acts on your show have rehearsed.

If two microphones are required for an act, as they are for Act #4 *(The Nelson Sisters)* in *The Rogers Revue* and Act #23 *(The Flamenco Troupe)* in *Celebrating Clarksville:*
    The sound assistant sets her microphone
    The MC introduces the act
        Meets the person who will be using his microphone
        as they arrive on-stage
        Helps them get settled
        Exits
    At the conclusion of the act, the MC enters applauding
        Retrieves his microphone
        Re-sets it at its usual place at the side of the stage
        Introduces the next act.

*By knowing exactly when and where props are to be placed, your stage manager
will soon learn how to set them quickly and with confidence.*
Whether or not you have a front curtain at your location doesn't matter.
*In fact, watching an efficient set-up for an act can be very interesting and enter-
taining in itself.*

COSTUME PARADE:—*Think Contrast!*

When lining up a costume parade, consider:

> How shy or bold is the wearer of the costume?
> How flamboyant, funny, scary, innovative is the costume?
> How tall or small is the model?

A SUGGESTED COSTUME PARADE OR FASHION SHOW LINE-UP:

First costume:	Attention-getter, strong colors
	Worn by a tall child or adult with a confident personality.
Second costume:	Contrasts strongly to the first costume
	Worn by a small, bold, child.
Third costume:	Funny or innovative
	Worn by a confident person, any size.
Middle models:	Shy
	Line them up from the shiest to the more confident.
	Costumes should build in interest from model to model.
Next to last:	Funniest or most innovative costume
	Worn by a confident person, any size.
Last costume:	Showiest, most flamboyant costume of all.
	Worn by an *"over-the-top"* personality type.

Presentation:

1. When a model is introduced, they make their entrance from launching pad #3.
2. They are instructed to walk diagonally from the rear wing and stop front and center on the curtain line.
3. While the narrator describes what they are wearing and who helped with the design or choice, the model turns slowly and shows the back of the costume.
4. When the narrator has completed the description, the model exits stage left.
5. The next model appears at the rear wing when their name is spoken, and so forth.

CHAPTER ELEVEN

THE SECOND REHEARSAL

The goal of the second rehearsal is to streamline and polish your show.

At the second rehearsal (the dress rehearsal) performers are asked to arrive in full costume. Their choice of costume may run the gamut from everyday clothing, to very elaborate, flamboyant creations.

If something is going to come apart or fall off, the director needs to know it now, at this rehearsal, while there is still time to make adjustments.

At the second rehearsal, the production team works from the same technical worksheet that was used for the first rehearsal. However, this time the show is done all in one piece. *(It is not divided up into sections, as it was before.)*
Performers are not dismissed after they perform, but stay for the entire rehearsal.

NO SPECTATORS PLEASE!

In the case of plays and other types of productions (which are rehearsed *many* times) guests are sometimes invited to the dress rehearsal. However, with this method, this rehearsal is only the second rehearsal where procedures and techniques are still being taught. For this reason, the second rehearsal for *Talent Shows the Kent Way* is a *closed* rehearsal. (No one is allowed in, except the performers and the production team.)

The objective is to give your cast and crew enough time to learn and *understand exactly what is expected of them,* so that when the audience *does* arrive, they will have the confidence to proudly present themselves at their most confident, poised and secure best!

CHECK LIST:

1. Set-up and check the sound system.
2. Turn on the stage and auditorium lighting.
3. Plug in and check the follow-spotlight.

4.   Account for all props.
5.   Make sure that the show's cassette tapes are:
        Cued up
        In order
        The first tape is loaded into the cassette player.

TAKING ATTENDANCE:

When performers arrive at the auditorium they are asked to stand in order of appearance *in three lines,* well away from the green-room area. *If an act is temporarily missing, a gap is left for them.*

Green-room Supervisor #1:	Is responsible for taking attendance for the performers who are in the first third of the show (the first line of performers).
Green-room Supervisor #2:	Is responsible for taking attendance for the middle third of the show (the second line of performers).
Green-room Supervisor #3:	Is responsible for taking attendance for the final third of the show (the third line of performers).

School Shows:

When the green-room supervisors take attendance and discover that someone is missing, the show coordinator assists by sending a messenger (not one of the green-room supervisors) to the missing person's classroom to try to find them. If they are absent, unfortunately, they will have to be deleted from the show.

All Shows:

In the green-room, two rows of performers will be seated and one row of performers will stand.

Originally, we had three rows of benches or chairs for the performers in the green-room. But we soon learned that the kids in the back row prefer to stand up to see the show.

Their turn to perform is imminent and they are energized.

They can see better if they are standing.

We, figured, if they want to stand up anyway, why have chairs or benches for them. So we eliminated the back row.

Please note: Acts that enter from the back of the auditorium (and crew members who also perform) are *not* seated in the green-room.

In sample show *The Rogers Revue,* Act #20 (the thirty swing dancers) and Act #25 (the seven teachers) are seated elsewhere.

ASSIGNING GREEN-ROOM SEATING:

The opening act stands at the beginning of the back row of performers.

They are followed by the next act on the bill (and so forth).

The closing act is seated farthest from the stage entrance.

The green-room traffic pattern winds in a <u>*backwards*</u> "S" shape:

←STAGE   *Opening Act:* **X**------------------------------------ ⟩

            ⟨ ------------------------------------**X** *Closing Act*

---

1. The standing back row moves toward the stage.
2. The seated middle row moves away from the stage and makes a U-turn at the end of the row (to become standees).
3. The seated front row (closest to the audience) moves toward the stage and makes a U-turn to become the middle row.

It's like playing the game *"musical chairs."* At the conclusion of an act, (during applause) performers move to the newly vacated seats.

The acts coming off stage, after they have performed, *go directly to the front row of benches or chairs.* (When the first act has finished performing, they go back to the green-room and sit next to the closing act.)

This procedure makes it possible for your performers to automatically be in the correct order, when it's time for the finale parade to begin.

THE FINALE PARADE WALK-THROUGH:

The director asks the curtain operator to open the curtain. Using a microphone, so that everyone can hear clearly, the director assigns *specific* walk-through tasks to the stage manager and the green-room supervisors.

The Stage Manager: When it's time to practice the walk-through, the stage manager goes to launching pad #3. This is where the performers enter for the finale parade. *(If there is no direct backstage access at your location, performers will enter from launching pad #1.)*

Green-room Supervisor #1 will stand at the head of the line of performers and send acts to the finale parade entry point on cue. (This will be discussed in more detail, later.)

Greenroom Supervisor #2 is in charge of helping performers stay in order when they return to the green-room. (During the finale parade, after bowing, performers exit down the center aisle.) When they get back to the green-room area, they are instructed to stay in the correct order and follow the same <u>backwards</u> 'S' traffic pattern every time.

Greenroom Supervisor #3 stands at the turning point (at the end of the center aisle, see *Auditorium set-up chart*) and reminds performers to go back to the green-room.

Note: Crew members who perform, do not take their bow during the finale parade. They are given recognition for performing as well as being a member of the crew (and take a bow) when the production team is acknowledged.

The finale walk-through familiarizes performers with the finale parade route.

After the bowing lesson, (the next step) the finale parade will be practiced, bows included.

The walk-through is practiced without music, so that the director's instructions and corrections can be clearly heard.

Variation on a circus style bow.
(A true circus bow: Arms extended horizontally).

THE FINALE PARADE

When taking their bows, performers are instructed to look directly at the audience, (1) into the left section (2) the right section (3) the center of the crowd (4) bow.

The objective is to make everyone in the audience feel
that they have been acknowledged and thanked individually.

BOWS AND BOW VARIATIONS:

After your performers have walked through the finale parade traffic pattern, the director demonstrates the finale bows.

The four-part bowing lesson:

1. *Enter:*

    The director explains that each act will make their entrance when told to do so by the stage manager.

    At the dress rehearsal, the director shouts, *"Go"* when it's time for the next act to enter. (Soon the stage manager will get the gist of how to time each act's entrance. When he or she feels confident enough to do so, the director asks him or her to take command.) Performers, who use props, should carry them when they bow. This reminds the audience of what they did on the show. For example, a trumpet player carries his or her trumpet. If there are more than six people in an act, they should divide their numbers and come out in sections (not more than six at a time; providing a better photo opportunity). Performers should plan ahead and decide who will enter first. Performers should enter quickly and with enthusiasm.

2. *Destination: The Curtain Line*

    Performers are instructed to come to a *complete* stop at the curtain line.

    Solo acts head for the curtain line's *center.*

    Duos space themselves; one on either side of the center tape, and so forth.

    Acts are asked to space themselves well, so that they create a visually pleasing, balanced picture that will look good on videotape or in photographs. *(The director helps each act make the necessary adjustments.)*

3. *Bow:*

    Acts who end their routine with a pose are asked to repeat the pose (if they want to) instead of taking a standard bow.

    Each act is encouraged to think of something unusual to do for their bow. For example:

    A martial arts demonstrator could replay his or her best move.

    If there is more than one person in an act, the act leader should signal their group in some way, so they know when to break their pose. For instance:

    Quietly say, *"break"*

    Snap their fingers…

4.   *Exit:*

> All acts exit down the center stairs.
>> It should be decided ahead of time who will go down the stairs first. It looks best if the center person in a group of three or more exits first and the others follow alternately.

The sound assistant and the show coordinator are asked to stand (one on either side), at the bottom of the center stairs and offer their assistance to the descending performers. This gracious gesture lends a sweet dignity to the proceedings and provides safety.

>> As soon as the previous act has taken their "bow" the stage manager immediately, sends the next act out.
>> Performers are asked to hurry down the center aisle, turn left at the end of the aisle and head back to the green-room.

REHEARSING THE PRODUCTION TEAM'S BOWS:

The house lights should be off and the curtain (if there is one) should be closed for this segment.

The MC is asked to read the last page of the cue sheet: (Example *The Rogers Revue*)
> *"Before our finale, let's take a moment to thank our production team for a great job."*

"At the spotlight back there—<u>KIM LEE AND RUMI SHARIF!</u>*"*
As they continue to focus on the MC, the two follow-spotlight operators wave from their positions beside the spotlight.

"On curtain—<u>DORA CUMMINGS!</u>*"*
The MC should step back, allowing space for the curtain operator to enter *(stage-right)*. The curtain operator bows center-stage and then returns to her post at the curtain control.

"Our stage manager—<u>FRANKIE BAHAR!</u>*"*
The stage manager enters from the opposite side of the stage *(stage-left)* and bows center-stage. He exits, goes to launching pad #3 and waits for the finale parade cue.

"Our sound assistant—Comedian—<u>YOLANDA GILLETTE</u>!*"*
The sound assistant goes from her position at the sound table, up the center-front stairs, takes a bow, goes back down the stairs and returns to her chair.

"Our green-room supervisors—<u>SHEEBA O'CONNOR, LATANIA LINCOLN AND VANESSA CRUZ</u>!*"*
Carrying their clipboards, they go up the side stairs, take a bow center-stage, go back down the side stairs to their finale parade posts.

"The show was produced by—Our Principal—<u>SAM GERSHWIN</u>!*"*
At this rehearsal, the spotlight operator is instructed to pretend to find the principal with the follow-spotlight. (At performances, so that he can be found quickly, he is spotted ahead of time.)

"Our Show Coordinator—PTA President—<u>TYRA WASHINGTON</u>!*"*
The spotlight operator finds her. She waves.

"Our Comedy Coach—<u>GRANDFATHER NAT EPSTEIN</u>!*"*
The spotlight operator finds him. He waves.

"Our Sound Technician—<u>JASMINE NOUY</u>!*"*
She stands next to the sound table, turns toward the audience and waves.

"Our show was directed by—<u>SOPHIA CASTILLANO</u>!*"*
The director, who is seated at the sound technician's table (during performances) stands, turns toward the audience and waves.

REHEARSING THE FINALE PARADE:

The director explains that after the closing act has performed and exited, everyone should listen for the cue:

<u>"BEFORE OUR FINALE…"</u>
This is the cue for *the first two acts* to go backstage to get ready for the finale parade.

The next cue to listen for is:

<u>"THE ENTIRE CAST IN REVIEW!"</u>

When hearing this cue:

1. The sound technician starts the music for the finale parade. (Up-tempo, easy to walk to, triumphant sounding music, is ideal.)
2. The curtain operator opens the curtain.
3. The stage manager sends the first act out for their bow.
4. The follow-spotlight pans from the MC to the first act.
5. The remaining performers stand up and start moving through the green-room traffic pattern.
6. In an orderly way, green-room supervisor #1 sends a continuous stream of performers back-stage, in single file.

As soon as the preceding act bows, the stage manager sends the next act out for their bow. This procedure is repeated until all of the acts on the show have bowed.

The curtain remains open throughout the entire finale parade.

The cue to close the curtain is a *visual* cue.
The curtain operator is instructed to close the curtain when she sees the *last person* in the *last act* begin to leave the stage.

As soon as the last act has bowed, the director takes command. Using microphone #2 and speaking from her position at the sound table, she says:

"The show wouldn't be complete without bringing our Master of Ceremonies back for a bow. Let's give a great big round of applause to—HEZEKIAH JONES!"

The MC enters (stage-right), takes a bow at center-stage and exits down the center stairs.

The director continues: "THANKS FOR BEING SUCH A WONDER-FUL AUDIENCE—GOOD NIGHT!"

The house light "ON" cue is: "Good night!" (or "Goodbye" if it's a morning show or matinee).

STEP 10: THE ENTIRE SHOW IS REHEARSED NON-STOP

The director introduces the MC.
All acts rehearse.
The production team is acknowledged.
The finale parade is practiced.
The MC takes a bow.
The director thanks and applauds the (imaginary) audience.

While this rehearsal is in progress, the director is very actively involved in bringing everyone up to performance level. He or she shouts out on-the-spot corrections and takes notes. At the end of this segment, the director reviews her notes and corrects problems that weren't dealt with during the non-stop phase of the rehearsal.

RULES OF BEHAVIOR:

1. Please wait your turn. Don't interrupt while the director is working with another act.
2. Don't talk while someone is performing; be attentive and supportive.
3. Genuine, heartfelt laughter is a delight. However, forced sarcastic laughter that belittles, is hurtful and unacceptable.
4. Never boo or jeer. Discouraging sounds of any sort are disheartening and are not to be tolerated (offenders will be excused from the show.)
5. No 'dirty' looks. If a member of an act makes a mistake while on stage his or her partners should not reproach them with disapproving looks.
6. The stage manager is in charge of the stage. Please cooperate by being quiet.
7. Leave the backstage area immediately after performing, unless otherwise instructed by the director.
8. No extra people are allowed backstage.
9. Don't touch props. The stage manager, the director and the act that uses the prop are the only people who are allowed to touch props.
10. Don't distract the MC or crew by talking to them during the show. They need to concentrate on their jobs so they don't miss their cues.
11. Don't ask the crew to make any changes. All changes must be cleared through the director.
12. The only time the center stairs are used for exits is during the finale parade.

ON-THE-SPOT CORRECTIONS MAY INCLUDE:

Problem: Performers not being centered on the stage.

Solution: The director points to the center-line while the act is in progress and asks them to adjust.

Problem: Performers, particularly dancers, who are too far back.

Solution: The director beckons them forward.

Problem: Dancers and movement acts who exit too soon.

Solution: The director asks them to 'freeze' (hold their pose) until the curtain is completely closed. If there is no curtain; hold their pose for the count of five and then run off-stage.

Problem: Something falls off during an act (a hat or a hair ribbon, for example).

Solution: Performers are instructed to pick up the dropped item, as quickly as possible. When something unintentionally drops onto the stage, the audience loses its focus. All eyes are on the hat, or whatever has fallen. For this reason, performers are asked to reclaim the audience's attention by (immediately) picking up whatever has fallen.

At the end of the second rehearsal:

1.   The director praises the performers and crew.
2.   Performers are asked to arrive at performances in make-up and costume, *completely ready* to perform.
3.   Performers are asked to conceal their costumes until it's their turn to perform; perhaps by wearing either a shawl or an oversized, borrowed shirt that buttons down the front (marked with the name of the act).
4.   Performers and crew are asked to arrive at the performance site, *promptly,* twenty minutes before the show is scheduled to begin
5.   The director tells everyone that *the show will start on time.*
6.   The majority of performers are dismissed.
7.   The acts that had difficulties and require extra attention are asked to stay.
8.   The director "irons out" any problems by either talking over the problem with the crew and performers or running through those particular acts again.

CHAPTER TWELVE

THE PERFORMANCES

SETTING UP:

The chairs at your performance site should be set up several hours ahead of time.

In an adjoining area:

A table for ticket sales should be in place.

A table for refreshment sales should be made available (if desired).

A table for souvenir sales should be made available (if desired).

CHECK LIST:

The director, the sound technician and the show coordinator arrive at the performance site at least an hour before the show is scheduled to begin.

The director:

1. Turns on the stage and auditorium lighting.
2. Plugs in and checks the follow-spotlight.
3. Checks to see that green-room seating is set up correctly.
4. Checks to see that the auditorium seating has been set up according to plan.
5. Reserves seats near the piano for accompanists.
6. Opens the front curtain. *The front curtain (if there is one) remains open until five minutes before show time.*

By leaving the curtain open until the "last minute", backstage mischief can be avoided. When the curtain finally <u>does</u> close, anticipation is heightened and everyone in the auditorium can feel a surge of excitement.

SOUND TECHNICIAN:

The sound technician sets up and checks the sound system.

COORDINATOR:

The coordinator helps the volunteers get organized:
    Ticket sales
    Refreshment and souvenir sales
    Video camera set-up
    Ushers/programs

SECURITY:

When security arrives, the director explains their duties to them.

STAGE MANAGER:

When the stage manager arrives, the director and the stage manager do a prop check.

EXIT DOORS:

Exit doors (on the sides of the performance site) should only be used when there is an emergency.

We suggest that you post signs on the side doors that say, *"Emergency Exit Only".*

The only door that should be used is the one that is at, or near, the rear of the auditorium.

STAGE FRIGHT:

Performers are told that having stage fright means that they truly care about the quality of their performance. They are advised to focus on one thing at a time:
    Take three very deep breaths.
    Listen for your cue.
    Make an enthusiastic entrance.
    Hit your mark (go to your starting place on the stage).
    Look for a friendly face
    Give your best.
    Enjoy your applause.

THE COUNT DOWN:

Fifteen minutes before show time:
    The director (using a microphone) asks the crew to go to their posts and the
    performers (who are assigned to the green-room) to go to their places.

Each green-room supervisor takes attendance for the performers in her section of the show, as usual.

Acts that are seated elsewhere are asked to check-in with green-room supervisor #1 as soon as they arrive, so that she can note that they are present.

Performers who are seated elsewhere:
Chaperoned large group acts (like the 30 swing dancers in *The Rogers Revue*) could wait in a room nearby. A designated scout would alert them when their performance time is drawing near (two acts ahead of time) so they can be in place at the back of the auditorium ready for their entrance cue well ahead time.

Large group, adult acts (like the seven teachers—*The Surfin' Sensations*) could also wait in a room nearby (if space in the auditorium is limited). As in the case above, a scout could inform them of their imminent cue.

Fourteen minutes before show time:
The director goes to the crew and asks if they have any last minute questions or concerns.
Shakes hands with each of them.
Praises them.
Thanks them for their support.

Ten minutes before show time:
The director thanks the green-room supervisors for their help.
Checks with them to make sure that all performers are present and accounted for.
Goes to the performers, praises, encourages and shakes hands with each one of them (if that's her style) and wishes them well.

Five minutes before show time:
The director asks the curtain operator to close the curtain (if there is a front curtain at the site).
Asks green-room supervisor #1 to send the first two acts backstage.
Checks with the MC to see if he or she has any last minute concerns or questions.
Praises him or her for their fine work.

At performances, the director sits at the sound technician's table, (between the sound technician and the sound technician's assistant) fairly close to the on-stage performers, as a kind of "security blanket". In this position, the director is *shielded by the piano, and is not seen by the audience. If a mishap occurs, <u>that</u> <u>they cannot deal with on their own,</u> performers know that they can depend on the director to help them.*

PERFORMANCE FORMAT:

1. The producer/sponsor welcomes the audience and introduces the MC. (*The house lights dim.*)
2. The MC introduces each act on the program, in succession.
3. The production team bows.
4. Finale parade.
    > The audience is encouraged to clap in time to the finale music.
    > Each act in succession takes a bow and exits down the center aisle, directly through the audience.
5. The MC takes a bow.
6. The director thanks the audience for their support.
    > The director and performers in the green-room give the audience a standing ovation.
    > The director says goodnight. (*The house lights go on.*)
7. The director and the coordinator make sure than *every* performer and crew member is praised after the show and that no one is left out. Hugs and compliments are everywhere!

PERFORMANCE NOTES:

During performances the director takes notes.
> The director continues to fine-tune the show as it progresses from one performance to the next.

LAST MINUTE REPLACEMENTS:

A *Talent Show the Kent Way* is a learning experience from start to finish; from the beginning of the audition to the conclusion of the final performance.

By allowing your performers to be in the auditorium for performances (where all the excitement and action is) they have the opportunity to see and feel their show develop and evolve.

Students have the chance to see themselves in context, as an integral part, necessary to the whole production. They observe how the laughter and applause varies from audience to audience and are able to provide team support for their fellow-performers. *(High fives abound!)* They get a chance to dream about how it might feel if they were to step into someone else's shoes and become a comedian, crew member, dancer, back-up singer…

On occasion, at the last minute, we have had to replace a member of the cast or crew when someone didn't show up. It is truly remarkable how observant the children in the green-room are, and how much information they absorb in so little time.

When suddenly put into the situation where a replacement is needed, (ten minutes before the show is scheduled to begin) someone from the green-room inevitably speaks up and says, *"I can do it!"* And the beautiful thing about it is, (with a little help from the director) *they can!*

THE CLARKSVILLE POLICE DEPARTMENT PROUDLY PRESENTS

CELEBRATING CLARKSVILLE

FEATURING POLICE PERSONNEL, SAFETY PATROL STUDENTS AND GUEST ARTISTS
COORDINATOR: OFFICER MARIA GUTIERREZ
DIRECTOR: DON ALEXANDER

FRIDAY & SATURDAY	MAY 24 & 25	CURTAIN 7 PM
SUNDAY	MAY 26	CURTAIN 2 PM

PROGRAM

MUSICAL DIRECTOR - BEBE WILLIAMS AND HIS LATIN/BLUES BAND	OVERTURE
COLOR GUARD - Evette Marx, Joseph Demos, Kim Lee, Clara Burke	PRESENTATION OF THE COLORS
MARIA ALEXANDER	NATIONAL ANTHEM
AGENT ED ZARNOW	MASTER OF CEREMONIES
JUMP MASTERS - Ivan Romanoff, Jenny Gutierrez, Wanda Hendrix, Suzie Hayakawa, Jose Lopez	ROPE SKIPPERS
GINGER JENKINS	TAP-DANCER
ANDY ANDERSON	COMEDIAN
THE WATSON SISTERS - Vanessa and Marie	VOCAL/DANCE ACT
OFFICER RICH DANIELS	HARMONICA
THE GUTIERREZ COUSINS - Debbie, Eve and Tish	IGOROT TRIBAL DANCERS
CARTER CHRISTIANSON	COMEDIAN
SUZANNE HUTTON	VOCALIST
GOTTA SHOUT - Cathy Kilbran, Barbara Bernstein, Marjorie McIntire, Dora and Mandy Duncan, Greta Myers, Sandra McBride, Francine Fraser, Katie Silva, Rosie Russell	CHEERLEADERS
OFFICER MICHAEL MICHAELSON	TUBA
TOMMY ZARNOW	COMEDIAN
NATALIE KAYE	VOCALIST
COUNTRY RHYTHM - Patty and Sandy Parton, Sonny Price, Francine Philips, Wanda Petri, Maria Pappas, Gertie Myers, Marg Smith, Annie Durante, Cher Kramer	CLOG DANCERS
OFFICER BENJAMIN BLAKE	MAGICIAN
TRUDY DEVENCENZO	VOCALIST
JOEY HENSON	COMEDIAN
COSTUMER THELMA HORNE - Models: Laura Horne, Bridgette Dubois, Francine Dauphin, Bette Bernstein, Cecilia Williams, Andrea Alexander, Mamie Sorenson, Amanda Harvey, Minny Tran, Paula Lucero, Ann Nguyen, Danielle Peterson	FASHION SHOW
OFFICER MARK ANDREWS	FIDDLER
HIP, SLICK & COOL - Terence Washington, Amanda Black, Miles Mercer, Sarah Nichols, Marty Michaelson, Cecily March	HIP-HOP DANCERS
MING & LONG - Joey and Timmy	COMEDIANS
OFFICER TOM HARMON	JUGGLER
AGENT ED ZARNOW	COMEDIAN
FLAMENCO GARCIA - Jose and Maria Garcia, Pedro Gomez, Lucia Cortez, Manuel Camacho, Lena Rodriguez, Toni Lucero, Juan Reyes, Margarite Ramirez, Constantine Aguilar	FLAMENCO TROUPE
JOIE DE VIVRE - Natasha Flynn, Alisha Connors, Elizabeth Marceau, Charlene Chapman, Jasmine Hope, Michelle Mathews	CANCAN
THE ENTIRE CAST	FINALE PARADE

CREDITS

BEBE WILLIAMS & HIS LATIN/BLUES BAND	COURTESY OF THE CLARKSVILLE CABARET
HARVEY BLOOM	BASS GUITAR
GINA DEVINCENZO	PERCUSSION
EZEKIEL FAIR	TRUMPET
SAM AMOS	TROMBONE
MC - AGENT ED ZARNOW	COMEDY COACH
RHONDA ROMANOFF, MARIA GUTIERREZ	CHOREOGRAPHERS
EMILIO BANDERAS	SOUND TECHNICIAN
CARTER CHRISTIANSON	SOUND ASSISTANT
MARJORIE CANNON, ELIZABETH LING, TISH COHEN	GREEN-ROOM SUPERVISORS
LORELEI GAIDA	STAGE MANAGER
HEIDI FOLTZ, HEATHER HAYAKAWA	SPOTLIGHT OPERATORS
MONIQUE BARDOT	SET DESIGN
OFFICER BEN BERNSTEIN, OFFICER MACK MCINTIRE	SET CONSTRUCTION
OFFICER RODNEY VIERRA	TICKET SALES
DIMITRI ROMANOFF	PROGRAM DESIGN
CLEOPATRA JONES	VIDEO CAMERA OPERATOR
MONIQUE DUBOIS, MIMI DAUPHIN	GREETERS/USHERS
GRETCHEN MYERS, CORRINE DUNCAN	REFRESHMENT SALES
ANDY KILBRAN, BENJAMIN HUTTON	SOUVENIR SALES
DAVID MCBRIDE, OFFICER MICHAEL PAPPAS	SECURITY
PAT RHEA, PHOENIX MCCOY	CUSTODIANS
PORTABLE SOUND SYSTEM	COURTESY OF BEBE WILLIAMS
FOLLOW-SPOTLIGHT	COURTESY OF THE CLARKSVILLE PLAYHOUSE
PHOTOFLOOD LAMPS	COURTESY OF KILBRAN PHOTOGRAPHY
TABLES AND CHAIRS	COURTESY OF CLARKSVILLE HIGH SCHOOL

To all you great parents, grandparents, teachers and friends,
thank you for your generous applause!

You are cordially invited to our after-show party.
Have your photo taken with a performer and/or a member of the production team.
Enjoy the happy sounds of BeBe Williams and his Latin/Blues Band.

Proceeds from ticket, refreshment, and souvenir sales will be contributed to
The Boys and Girls Club of Clarksville.

APPLAUSE, PRAISE, TRIUMPH!
Various people, especially your coordinator and director,
may be given flowers in recognition for their contribution to the show.
The ideal time for this presentation to occur is
during the production team bow segment; just before the finale parade.

A MINI MEMOIR

JACKIE'S THEATRICAL EXPERIENCE:

Vancouver, Canada

Jackie began her theatrical studies (voice and stage deportment) at age six with Dayde Harvey-Rutherford, a well-known producer/director of high-quality shows involving children. Mrs. Rutherford conveyed to Jackie her deep love and respect for the audience and the feeling that every detail of a performer's presentation is significant.

A few months after her studies began, Mrs. Rutherford invited Jackie to sing at a convention for the Associated Press at Vancouver's *Hotel Georgia* and both of Jackie's parents came to see her perform. Her father, Cyril Ernest Pheby, (pronounced Feebee) later commented in his memoirs, *"It was obvious to Beatrice (Jackie's mother) and myself that Jackie had the spark that it takes to win a discerning audience. We were delighted!"*

When Jackie was seven-years-old, her dad put an act together and named it, *"Sweethearts on Parade"*. The act consisted of *"The Curly Tops"*, three girls who tap-danced, sang and played accordions and saxophones and Jackie, who performed as the troupe's Mistress of Ceremonies, stand-up comic and lead singer. Two years later, Jackie's sister Marilyn, joined the act.

REVIEW:

"The Mandarin Supper Club will present the famous Vancouver act that has made such a name for itself and Vancouver along the entire coast. It is "Sweethearts on Parade" which features five little girls who sing, dance and play several musical instruments. Presented and trained by Cyril Pheby they present a miniature musical revue that has had critics applauding wherever they have appeared."

THE VANCOUVER DAILY PROVINCE

<u>SWEETHEARTS ON PARADE</u>

The Curly Tops, pictured with saxophones:
Sheila Honey, Cherie Honey and Nelwyn Nesbit.
Marilyn, with trumpet and Jackie, with trombone.

The Pheby Sisters made their debut at The *Edison Theater* in New Westminster, British Columbia, When Jackie was ten and Marilyn was eleven-years-old. In preparation, Jackie learned to play the soprano saxophone. Her teacher was John Bowman (the orchestra leader at Vancouver's *Beacon Theater*). Marilyn continued to study with well-known trumpeter, Tug Wilson. Jackie and Marilyn performed as a vocal/instrumental sister-act for twelve years.

THE PHEBY SISTERS

THEATRICAL AGENTS:

Vancouver:	Gerry Lancaster, Fred Bass and Charlie Nelson.
Seattle:	Joe Daniels and Len Mantel handled their more prestigious bookings that included: *The Beacon Theater* and *The Cave Supper Club* in Vancouver, *The Palomar Theater* in Seattle and *The Capital Theater* in Portland.
Des Moines:	Irving Grossman booked them onto *International Harvester* tours and grandstand shows throughout the mid-west.
Chicago:	Sam Roberts and Goldie Cohen handled most of their Chicago work that included conventions in many of Chicago's major hotels. Len Fisher booked them on *The Red Hot and Beautiful* tour that included airbases in Louisiana, Kansas, Texas and New Mexico.
Montreal:	Fred Norman handled their nightclub work in and around Quebec City and Montreal.
New York:	Matty Rosen booked them into the *Orpheum* and *Jefferson Theaters*, Eddie Smith booked them into the *Palace Theater*, Nat Abramson was their agent for *Cunard Cruises*.
World Tours:	Charlie Burgess and Bert Wishnew, (U.S.O. Shows, New York City office) booked Jackie and Marilyn on tours to Japan, Korea, Germany, France, Austria, Algeria, Libya, Morocco, Iceland, Greenland and Labrador.

REVIEWS:

Les soeurs Pheby, chanteuses et musiciennes extraordinaires. MONTREAL MATIN

Combining fresh young personalities with "sock" singing and musical ability, the Pheby Sisters are far and away the most refreshing interlude in any program they play. Marilyn plays a trumpet that is the envy of male musicians many years her elder, while Jackie plays soprano sax in a manner reminiscent of the "daddy" of them all, Sidney Bechet.
CENTERVILLE, IOWEGIAN

Success Story—"We're going to play the Palace!" This remark by a vaudeville performer means reaching the ultimate in the business. Playing the Palace is like reaching Mecca or seeing Naples before dying. It will come true next spring for two Vancouver girls, pretty and statuesque musicians. They are the Pheby Sisters, Jackie and Marilyn.
VANCOUVER DAILY PROVINCE

MARRIAGE:

In rehearsals for a USO tour to the Arctic, Jackie and Marilyn met their future husbands. After a two-week whirlwind courtship, Marilyn married trumpet player, Bob Schreffler. When the tour ended, Jackie married bass player, Danny Kent.

The Schreffler newly-weds moved to Chicago (Bob's hometown) and the Kent newly-weds stayed in New York City.

Danny was born in Paris, France. He went to *Dartington Hall*, a progressive boarding school in Totnes, Devon, England and *Pickering College*, a prep school, in Newmarket, Ontario, Canada. He has a BA from *Yale*, an MA from *Columbia* and a teaching credential in music

DANNY KENT

DANNY'S CAREER HIGHLIGHTS:

Toured with big bands:	Ray McKinley, Tommy Tucker, Richard Maltby, Larry Clinton…
Roseland Ballroom, New York City:	The Warren Covington Orchestra
Tavern on the Green, New York City:	The Warren Covington Orchestra
Greek parties and weddings:	The Gus Vali Orchestra
Jewish weddings and bar mitzvahs:	The Harry Frank Orchestra
Recorded with:	Eduardo's Mambos Modernos
Sat in with jazz great:	Charlie Parker
Park Hotel, Washington, D.C:	Played for and jammed with, Mel Torme
Julius Monk's Upstairs at the Downstairs, New York City:	Worked with Hubbel Pierce and Lovelady Powell
Far East, Europe, N.E. Air Command:	USO Shows.

Several months after Jackie and Danny were married, Charlie Burgess, the musical director for USO Shows contacted Jackie and said, *"If you'll do a solo singing act and learn to play the drums, so that you can double in the show band, I'll send you and Danny out on tour together."* Jackie jumped at the chance and scrambled to get ready. She studied jazz drumming with Sonny Igoe and Latin percussion with Sam Ulano. Jackie and Danny toured the world for a decade, practically non-stop.

JACKIE KENT

REVIEW:

"Zingiest drummer who ever wielded a stick, curvaceous Jackie Kent is currently enchanting audiences all over the world."

STARS AND STRIPES, FRANKFURT, GERMANY

JACKIE & DANNY'S U.S.O. TOURS:

The Far East:	Japan, Korea, Vietnam, Thailand, Taiwan, the Philippines, Guam, Midway, Hawaii.
Europe:	Germany, France, Italy, and Spain.
N.E. Air Command:	Iceland, Greenland, Labrador, Newfoundland.
Alaska:	Alaska and the Aleutian Islands.
Caribbean:	Panama, Guantanamo Bay, Cuba, Bermuda, and Puerto Rico.
Mediterranean:	Turkey, Greece, Saudi Arabia, Iran, Ethiopia, and Pakistan.

After many years of world tours, (the public relations department of U.S.O.'s New York office estimated that Jackie and Danny had logged well over a million miles) the Kents decided to settle down and start a family. They were blessed with three beautiful baby girls; Linda, Lizette and Madeleine.

For seven years, Danny taught music at *Mahoney Junior High School* in South Portland, Maine. During Danny's time there, Mr. Lancaster, Mahoney's principal, asked him to organize a talent show. Danny asked Jackie to help him put it together. (Jackie lined up the show and instructed the stage crew.)

When each of his daughters reached age four, Danny began their musical education by teaching them how to play the soprano recorder (a flute-like, medieval instrument). After a time, when they became more proficient, Danny wrote five-part arrangements of compositions by Bach, Mozart, Corelli and Teleman, and the whole family played recorders together.

KENT PUPPET SHOWS:

While living in South Portland, Maine, Jackie volunteered to help plan an activity for a Halloween Carnival at her children's school, *Kaler Elementary*. She went to the local library, looked at lists of possibilities and decided on a puppet show. The books she borrowed were of tremendous help. Jackie wrote two scripts and indicated what kind of music and sound effects she wanted. She hand-made a cast of puppet characters and built a puppet stage out of pegboard, tied together with shoelaces and draped with black fabric.

Danny became very interested in the project and made a sound track on a *Sony*, reel-to-reel, tape recorder. The whole family got involved and recorded a variety of voices for the various puppet characters that had been created.

The show at *Kaler* was a huge success. The librarian at *Mahoney Junior High School* told Jackie about an organization called, *Puppeteers of America* and through that organization she met the brilliant puppet maker (and illustrator of this book) *Michael Hatch*. Michael arranged for Jackie to perform at a ladies' luncheon, her first professional puppet show. Jackie contacted elementary schools, libraries and recreation centers and booked performances in and around Portland. She also joined *The New England Guild of Puppetry* and *The Union Internationale de la Marionette*.

REVIEW:

Pert Jackie has been a puppeteer for a year now. Jackie has a repertoire: There's "Bad Luck, Good Luck", "The Three Billy Goats Gruff", "Beauty and the Beast", among others. Husband Danny's know-how in taping music and sound effects is also used in the show, while Jackie, who is heard but not seen, manipulates the puppets. The Kents have enough records and sound effects equipment in the house to duplicate horses galloping and whinnying, pigs squealing, donkeys braying, plus storms at sea, bells ringing or anything that might come up in the scripts.

MAINE SUNDAY TELEGRAM

CAREER HIGHLIGHTS:

Jordan Marsh Department Store:	South Portland, Maine
The Puppet Showplace:	Brookline, Massachusetts
The Balboa Park Puppet Theater:	San Diego, California
Wild Animal Park:	San Diego, California
Seaport Village:	San Diego, California
Nordstrom Department Stores:	San Diego, California; Horton Plaza, Fashion Valley, North County Fair
Elementary School Assemblies:	Los Angeles, Orange, Riverside, San Bernardino, Imperial and San Diego Counties.

TALENT SHOW DIRECTING:

What began as a willingness to help out at their children's school, blossomed into a very fulfilling career!

A few months after the Kent family's arrival in California, Danny attended a *Parent Club* meeting at *Allen Elementary School* (his daughters' school) in Bonita, near San Diego. A talent show was being planned and a director was needed. Danny asked Jackie if she would be willing to co-direct with him and she said *"yes"* and they volunteered. The total number of students who signed-up for their first show at *Allen School* was 38. The show was such a happy event, that the *Parent Club* invited them back to direct the following year. When it was time for *Allen School's* second annual talent show, participation doubled. By the time Jackie and Danny returned to direct for the third year in succession, involvement had expanded considerably and 130 students signed up. Word got around and invitations to direct children's talent shows all over San Diego County started pouring in.

LINDA KENT

Whenever a talent show was scheduled at *Allen School,* the Kent children got involved too.

Linda was the show-drummer.

LIZETTE KENT

Lizette sang and played trombone on a heartfelt rendition of *"Maybe"* from the Broadway show *"Annie".*

Madeleine played saxophone and "knocked the family out" with her *Sam Butera* type sound on *"Tequila"*.

MADELEINE KENT

THE KENT'S PORTABLE SOUND SYSTEM:

The portable sound system that served the Kents well for many years:
    Amplifier—*TOA model MX-401*
    Two speakers—*Peavey Mini-monitors*
    Two microphones—*Shure cardioid*

AUTHORS: JACKIE & DANNY KENT

GRATEFULLY THANK AND ACKNOWLEDGE:

Lizette Kent:	Editor
Michael Hatch:	Illustrator
Valerie Haas:	Publishing service associate
June Bohler:	Data processor
Linda Kent:	Comments and suggestions
Madeleine Kent:	Comments and suggestions

PHOTO CREDIT:

Artone Studios:	Vancouver, Canada	*Sweethearts on Parade* . . . .Page 126
Maurice Seymour:	Chicago	*The Pheby Sisters* . . . . . . .Page 127
Maurice Seymour:	New York	*Danny Kent* . . . . .Page 128
Maurice Seymour:	New York	*Jackie Kent* . . . . .Page 130
Robert Burroughs:	San Diego	*Linda Kent* . . . . .Page 133
Robert Burroughs:	San Diego	*Lizette Kent* . . . . .Page 133
Robert Burroughs:	San Diego	*Madeleine Kent* . . . . .Page 134
Robert Burroughs:	San Diego	*Jackie & Danny Kent* . . . . .Page 134

GLOSSARY

Accompanist:	One who gives musical support.
Act:	Any of the separate performances in a variety show. An act can consist of either one or two people or a group of people who dance, sing, play musical instruments, do comedy or a novelty presentation; (something unusual like yo-yo tricks, a martial arts demonstration…)
Adapter clip:	A screw-on attachment that goes between a microphone stand and a microphone. This device makes it possible to remove the microphone from the stand, quickly and easily.
Assembly:	A performance for students and teachers.
Assisting adults:	Show coordinator, director, sound technician.
Attack:	The onset of a desired sound.
Audition:	The first of the three production sessions in the Kent method of directing talent shows. The director sees each act perform and then decides where on the program to place them.
Backstage:	Parts of the stage that are unseen by the audience.
Bar:	A section into which a piece of music is divided.
Break-dance:	Popular street dance that includes back spins.
Cast:	The performers, as distinguished from the crew.
Character:	Collective qualities that distinguish a person's mannerisms, tone of voice, inflection, accent…
Chinese ribbon dance:	A dance that features ribbon streamers. Ribbon streamers are about ten feet long and make large, swirling patterns as dancers glide and turn, creating a bold, beautiful visual effect. (They can usually be found where educational supplies are sold; in the active play department.)
Choreographer:	One who designs or arranges a dance.
Chutzpah:	Confidently assertive, adventurous, brave; (pronounced, hutzpa).
Color guard:	A small group of people who present the colors (flag); a short patriotic ceremony.

Combining acts:	At the discretion of the director, one or more acts of a similar type may be joined together, forming a larger act.
Comedian:	A humorous entertainer.
Comedy coach:	A person who has a flair for instructing others in the art of presenting amusing visual (sight gags) or spoken material (jokes, monologues…) to an audience.
Comic:	A funny person (interchangeable with comedian).
Contact person:	Well informed person who has the authority to make decisions.
Crew:	The stage manager, green-room supervisors, sound technician's assistant, curtain operator, follow-spotlight operators.
Cue:	Dialogue or action that is the signal for the working of lights, curtain, music, etc. (The MC's introduction to an act ends with a cue; the name of the act).
Cue sheet:	A list of introductions that the MC reads when presenting acts to the audience.
Cue up:	Playing, then slightly rewinding a cassette tape, so that the desired music or sound effect will be heard without delay.
Curtain cue:	Dialogue, action or music that is the signal for the curtain to open or close.
Delivery:	Manner of speaking or performing.
Del Mar Fair:	*Recently re-named San Diego County Fair;* An annual event in the San Diego area known for its 4-H exhibits, amusement rides, local talent and grandstand shows that feature internationally famous entertainers.
Fade out ending:	The volume of the music is gradually decreased.
Family events:	Wedding receptions, reunions, birthday parties…
Festival:	Day of celebration that features cultural events.
Fifties dance:	A dance that was popular during the decade: 1950-1959.
Finale parade:	The reappearance and bows of the cast, accompanied by happy music in a fast, easy to walk and applaud to tempo. Music choice suggestions: A samba, or something triumphant sounding like the theme from the Olympics.
Flat:	Flat scenery on a frame.
Follow-spotlight:	A movable spotlight.
Gel:	A colored transparent gelatin based, paper-like material, which is placed over the lens of a theatrical light.

Green-room:	An area where performers wait before going on stage.
House lights:	The lights in the audience part of a theater or auditorium.
Igorot tribal dance:	A dance that originated in the Philippine Islands.
Impersonator:	One who pretends to be another person or character. Usually someone famous like: *President Lincoln, Cher, Tina Turner...*
Innovate:	Bring in new methods or ideas.
In sequence:	Acts rehearse in succession, according to the show's line-up (order of appearance on the program). *The 2ⁿᵈ rehearsal must be done in sequence.*
Iris control:	The knob on a follow-spotlight that regulates the admission of light to the lens.
Jump-the-gun:	Begin prematurely.
Key:	System of notes related to each other and based on a particular note. For example: *Key of C major.*
Launching pad:	An area at the side of the stage, defined by masking tape (placed 3' back from the sight line—parallel to the side wall). This marking lets performers know where to stand before they are introduced and prevents them from being seen by the audience ahead of time.
Lens:	A piece of transparent glass with one side curved for concentrating light-rays.
Line-up:	The order of the acts on a variety/talent show.
Live:	Heard or seen at the time of the performance, as opposed to pre-recorded.
Live music:	Music that is performed while the audience is present as opposed to pre-recorded music.
Lyrics:	Words of a song
MC:	Master or Mistress of Ceremonies. The person who introduces performers to the audience.
Media:	Mass communication.
Motivator:	A person who stimulates the interest of another.
Musical director:	A skilled musician who helps to choose and/or transpose music for performers who require assistance. Usually serves as an accompanist or band leader.
Music cue:	Dialogue or action that is the signal for music to start or stop.
Novelty act:	A type of variety show presentation other than dancing, singing, instrumental or comedy.

Out-of-sequence:	The 1st rehearsal is conducted according to the order of appearance of the acts on the program. However, acts made up of large groups of people or acts with scheduling problems, can be seen by the director at a different time or out-of-sequence. *This applies to the 1st rehearsal only.*
Pace:	Rate of movement or progression. The un-interrupted pace of the show, *the show keeps moving, without delays.*
Painter's masking tape:	Masking tape that is less adhesive than ordinary masking tape. It is not supposed to remove varnish or paint when lifted off.
Pan:	Move a camera or spotlight horizontally to follow a traveling performer across the stage, as distinguished from tilting a camera or spotlight up and down.
Patch into:	To connect electronically.
Placement code:	A system of evaluating acts so that they will be sensitively positioned on the program and shown off to their best advantage.
Pose-and-freeze:	An applause-stimulating ending for an act, usually movement or dance.
Premiss:	The essence of a joke or comedy sketch. The basic or indispensable element.
Press release:	Statement issued to the media; newspapers, television and radio. Contains information about forthcoming performances that are *open to the public;* name of the show, location, show times, price of admission, phone, fax and/or e-mail numbers of the contact person.
Production team:	Consists of assisting adults, crew and MC. *Assisting adults:* Show coordinator, director, and sound technician. *Crew:* Stage manager, green-room supervisors, sound technician's assistant, curtain operator, follow-spotlight operators.
Projection booth:	An elevated room at the back of a theater or auditorium. A film projector or follow-spotlight is operated from this location.
Prop:	Abbreviation for property. Any moveable article used in an act. For example: A chair, music stand, magician's table…
Proscenium:	The structure that is in front of the curtain; the enclosing arch or rectangle that frames the stage.

Public relations:	Promotion of a public image.
Punch-line:	Words giving the point of a joke or story.
R&B:	Rhythm and Blues. Popular music with blues themes and a strong rhythm.
Recast:	Cast again, put into a new form. Performers are given an alternate choice; they are given the opportunity to either join the comedy team or be in the costume parade.
Recital:	A program that focuses on one type of performance only; dance, classical musicianship…
Rhythm:	Periodical accent and the duration of notes in music, especially as beats in a bar. Type of structure formed by this *(samba rhythm)*.
Routine:	Unvarying performance of an act.
Samba:	Dance of Brazilian origin.
Screen:	Check for inappropriate content.
Script:	Text for comedians to memorize.
Sell:	Present enthusiastically.
Set props:	Place performing equipment precisely on the stage, ready for use.
Set-ups:	Getting ready for an act's entrance. Placing what is needed for a performer's use; microphone, table…
Sight-line:	The point at which performers are visible to the audience.
Sketch:	An act in the form of a very short play, usually comedy. Sometimes called by amateurs, a skit.
Spaced:	Spread out evenly.
Stage-left:	The left side for the performer, facing the audience.
Stage-right:	The right side for the performer, facing the audience.
Standard music:	Music that withstands the test of time. For example: *"Autumn Leaves"*.
Stand-up comedian:	A person who tells jokes or relates humorous anecdotes to an audience.
Stopwatch:	A watch that can be stopped and started. It is used to time musical introductions, the length of each act and prop set-ups.
Straight man:	A performer (male or female) who acts as a stooge for a comedian.
Syncopate:	Displace the beats or accents in music.
Technical worksheet:	Each crew member works from a copy of the technical worksheet. It lists act numbers, curtain cues, prop set-ups,

microphone set-ups and whether or not an act uses live or taped accompaniment.

Tempo: Speed at which music is or should be played.

Throw-away line: A sentence or phrase that is said while the applause is subsiding. It doesn't matter if it is actually heard or not.

Timing: Interplay or give-and-take between a performer and the audience, especially when humor is involved.

Top-40: The forty most popular songs of the day.

Transpose: Put music into a different key.

Traveling: Moving across or back and forth on a stage as distinguished from moving in place.

Trick: Feat of skill or dexterity.

Up-tempo: A faster speed at which music can be played.

Visual cue: A move, gesture or pose that the crew watches for. It signals when to close the curtain, fade-out the music...

Vocal range: The lowest note to the highest note that a person can sing without straining.

Wings: The concealed place where a performer waits (at the side of a stage) just before making their entrance.

INDEX

A

accompanist, 35, 54-55, 100, 137, 139

act
  alternate choice, 52
  categories, 33, 66
  closing, 8, 67-68, 108, 113
  dangerous, 63
  naming, 54
  opening, 66-69
  silent, music for, 62

acts, too few
  too many, 38

adults, 8, 10, 12-13, 28, 37, 41, 137, 140

agility, 58

all-purpose show, 27, 36

amateur performers, 52

amplifier, 21, 134

ante-pro lights, 22, 97

applause, 3, 7-8, 47, 77, 96, 108, 114, 118, 120, 142

artistic ability, 5

assembly, 137

assist performers, 46

assisting adults, 8, 13, 137, 140

attack, sound, 56

attention, 8, 23, 47, 53, 59, 66, 68-69, 77, 90, 92, 95-96, 98, 116

audience, comfort
  space, 24, 45, 82

audition
  all-purpose, 36, 63
  order of, 46

  preparation, 25
  sample, 53
  setting up, 45

auditorium set-up chart, 81

B

back boundary, stage, 82

backstage, 12-13, 33, 89-91, 96, 98, 102, 109, 113-115, 117, 119, 137

backdrop, 20, 41, 79-80, 82

back wall, 20

beats, counting, 53

beginning, strong, 1, 44, 55

behavior, rules of, 115

border lights, 22, 97

boundaries, 44, 79, 82, 99

bows, performer
  production team, 106, 112, 120
  variations, 111

brackets, curtain cue code, 90

building routines, 62

C

cartoonists, advice for, 61

cassette tape, 53, 56, 86, 91-92, 100, 138

cast, 5, 7, 52, 102, 106, 113, 121, 131, 137-138, 141

categories of acts, 33, 66

CD player, 44-45

center stage, 52, 56, 79, 95

character, 4, 52, 137, 139

charisma, 58

"…Good my lord, will you see the players well bestowed? Do you hear? Let them be well used for they are the abstract and brief chronicles of the time…"

WILLIAM SHAKESPEARE—HAMLET

0-595-29486-3

Made in the USA
Lexington, KY
22 September 2012